*R*evelation
S UBU D

*One man's extraordinary story,
and a message for all mankind*

*R*evelation
S UBU D

One man's extraordinary story,
and a message for all mankind

Emmanuel Elliott

DAWN CHORUS
Publishers
Los Angeles • London

First published in 1991 by
DAWN CHORUS
419 N. Larchmont Blvd.
Suite 22
Los Angeles, Ca. 90004

Printed in tne United States of America

Library of Congress Catalog Card No. 91-70445

ISBN 0-9628922-0-3

This book has been written with all the sincerity I can muster, for *all* sincere seekers of the way, the truth, and the life.

It is dedicated to Suzanna, my beloved wife, who has not only shared in living this story but is willing that it should be told.

Acknowledgements

Many Subud friends encouraged me in writing this book, too many to name, and I am grateful to them all.

My particular thanks to Emma Bragdon, Maria Contessa, Danielle Elaine, Rohana Goodale, Michael Menduno, Antony Taylor, and Robert Wilton for their special input along the way.

My thanks also to editor Diane Chalfant for her invaluable objectivity, and to Subud Publications International for permission to quote from Bapak's talks.

Most of all, I wish to express my heartfelt gratitude to Susannah Clarke for her inspired editorial "midwifery," and to Rashid Butte for his unflagging belief in this project. Their loving support helped to sustain my courage and commitment in recording the process described in these pages.

As a member of the Subud International Cultural Association, I owe a special debt of gratitude to SICA (USA) for its support of this project.

CONTENTS

*In Christianity it has been said that Christ has already come down to earth. This is not the Christ that you see in the pictures; for he has come down to **human beings themselves** at this time…*

Indeed, in Christianity it has become known that something will arise in the East that signals the return of Jesus Christ to earth… and from here it will spread.

—Bapak Muhammad Subuh Sumohadiwidjojo

In Retrospect

For thirty-three years I have been a follower of the way of Subud, a spiritual awakening made newly available to mankind in our era through an Indonesian, one Bapak Muhammad Subuh Sumohadiwidjojo, who died in 1987.

Throughout those years I have witnessed the Subud contact putting both Christians and Muslims, as well as Buddhists, Jews, Hindus, and even atheists and agnostics, in touch with their own inner being and, in the process, making the spiritual life and the brotherhood of man a living reality.

Having for so long delighted in recognizing the light of truth shining through all the principal religions, I had left my Christian conditioning far behind by the time the series of extraordinary experiences related in this book began. Furthermore, partly because Bapak— the first man to receive the spiritual exercise of Subud—had been born a Muslim, I had come to feel that Christ had had his day; that he had been a messenger for another time.

That is, until relatively recently.

Late in 1989, quite unexpectedly and in rather dramatic circumstances during a visit to Medugorje, Yugoslavia, I was brought to see that Christ is not exactly the obsolete figure I had assumed him to be: that in fact the spiritual exercise of Subud is a manifestation of his Second Coming.

But perhaps I should start at the beginning!

PART I. JOURNEY TO THE LIGHT

Hold Everything!

L ondon, England, 1957. Autumn was fast approaching, as was my twenty-first birthday, and I was a sergeant in the Royal Air Force, a member of the personal staff of the Commander-in-Chief, Fighter Command. My immediate boss was Squadron Leader Roy H. Crompton. Quite apart from our normal working relationship, Roy and I had for some time shared common ground of a less official nature: the search for truth. We had gotten into the habit of comparing notes on the latest mystical literature we came across, discussion groups we attended, and so on. This sharing of interests was of great value to us both.

My own quest had begun in earnest around the age of eighteen. Following an adverse reaction in my early teens against a rather rigid Christian upbringing, I struggled with the idea that any one religion could lay sole claim to spiritual reality when generations of sincere people were born into such a diversity of religious and cultural environments. Surely the answer had to be much deeper than the dogmatic, superficial exclusivity of one group or another. Was it not possible that all the great religions, all true ways to spiritual knowledge, had sprung from the same pure source to which they were all aspiring to return?

An early breakthrough was my discovery in the public library of a slim volume on Buddhism, by Christmas Humphries. I can still remember the excitement with which I devoured this little book. It seemed to throw open a great window in my mind. After visiting a London monastery, I went on to read many other books on Buddhism, as well as the writings of Sufi, Jewish, and Hindu mystics. The works of Krishnamurti, Rudolph Steiner, Gurdjieff, and Ouspensky also played a part in broadening my perception. But the most memorable impression of all from that period was a story of Ramakrishna. This nineteenth century Indian saint was moved to devote three months respectively to the practice of each of the major world religions. At the end of this experiment he was able to bear witness that in essence they were all the same, that each led to the same inner bliss.

My friend was pursuing his own lines of inquiry, of course, and it was not unusual, when time allowed, for us to interrupt the working day with an exchange of ideas. What was unusual, however, was the light in Roy's eyes one morning when he bounced into the office and said, "Hold everything!" He could hardly contain his enthusiasm. "I had a telephone call last night from Michael Scott, an old friend of mine now living in Tangiers. He wanted me to know about a visit to England by a Javanese master called Bapak. According to Michael, this man is able to put people directly in touch with the power of God within themselves. He's been staying at the Gurdjieff Institute near Richmond, run by J.G. Bennett."

It transpired that Bapak had spent several weeks at Coombe Springs in Surrey as the guest of John Bennett, a leading figure in the movement dedicated to the Gurdjieff method of working upon the self. It seemed that the man from Indonesia had created something of a spiritual whirlwind by introducing Bennett and hundreds of fellow Gurdjieff followers to a new spiritual way, a uniquely personal inner awakening.

There was something compelling about this report. Within days, Roy and I were among a crowd gathered at Coombe Springs to hear Mr. Bennett talk about something called Subud. Subud, it seemed, was the name of the movement rapidly gaining ground in the West in the wake of Bapak's recent first visit to this hemisphere.

Bennett told us about the early life of Bapak himself, and how he had received the powerful spiritual vibration now causing so much interest and excitement in this quiet corner of Surrey.

"The transmission of this inner contact from one person to another is called the *opening*," Bennett explained. "After being opened you will be able to experience a spontaneous and ongoing spiritual exercise."

As he spoke I felt touched and calmed inside. I somehow knew that this was "it," and all my questioning fell away. A week later, returning in company with a train car half full of other inquirers, I found it hard to understand why the others seemed to need to debate and analyze what Subud was all about. Although characteristically I would have been active in such a discussion, now it was enough for me to sit quietly in tune with the inner certainty that possessed me.

As proof of our sincerity, and to give us time to find out all we could about Subud, we were required to wait three months before being opened. It was a period that passed all too slowly for me. But pass it did, and on January 18, 1958, I made my way back down to Coombe Springs from North London for the big event. My feelings were a mixture of nervousness and keen anticipation.

I was shown into a small room already occupied by three or four Subud members, all men. There I was asked to remove my jacket, shoes and tie. We were joined by a young Indonesian named Sjafrudin, who was one of Bapak's key helpers in the West at that time. One of the men read a short statement explaining that they were there as witnesses to my wish to worship God. He went on to explain that it was only necessary for me to relax without concentrating my thought, and then said, "Begin."

The others began to move slowly around the room, some of them singing in a gentle, highly individual way. I felt impatient to join in. To my surprise and slight irritation, however, my knees kept threatening to give way. Again and again I forced myself to straighten up to be ready to begin my spiritual exercise. Eventually it occurred to me that my legs knew, better than my mind, that my exercise had begun and I decided to allow my legs to have their own way. Immediately, and unexpectedly, I fell to my knees in a spontaneous movement of worship and surrender.

My life was never to be the same again. My *Subud* life had begun.

What Is Subud?

Before continuing with my personal story and the remarkable events that lay ahead, I will pause to explain more about Subud itself, about the man who founded it, and about the international spiritual association that bears its name.

What exactly is Subud? Subud is a way of worship and purification, a way of self-realization based upon total surrender to almighty God. It is a way that progresses of itself from a source deep within a person's inner being, as a result of nothing less than a direct personal contact with the power of God.

The term *Subud* is a contraction of three Sanskrit words: *Susila, Budhi,* and *Dharma*—which can be summarized to mean "right living from within according to the will of God." Another explanation is that when the name was first received it brought its own meaning with it, namely, "from God, through God, back to God."

But the particular concept of God and how we define God is not itself important to the experience of Subud. In fact, those uncomfortable with concepts like God and will of God might well express this same reality in terms of their own choosing and understanding. They might speak of harmonizing with the vital essence at the heart of all creation; of uniting with that love and light in which all is one; of merging with the life that is both unimaginably vast and universal and at the same time inexpressibly personal and near.

At the heart of Subud is the *latihan kejiwaan,* two Indonesian words that simply mean "spiritual exercise." Exercise (or "training") is the English word that comes closest to expressing the meaning of the Indonesian word latihan, although most Subud people still prefer to use the original word latihan.

This spiritual exercise, or latihan, was first received by Muhammad Subuh Sumohadiwidjojo, the man now known around the world simply as Bapak, the Indonesian word for father or respected older man. (The name Subuh, incidentally, means "dawn" and is not etymologically connected with the word "Subud.")

For the purposes of this book, my treatment of Bapak's life will cover only the basic essentials. For the full story I would refer the reader to Bapak's *Autobiography,* published posthumously at his request by Subud Publications International, England.

Bapak was born at dawn on June 22, 1901, and died at dawn on June 23, 1987. His birth was preceded and accompanied by many signs and portents, and from his earliest days it was clear that he was indeed a man of destiny.

Bapak was drawn from an early age to the quest for the perfect life, but was told by local gurus that he already carried within himself that which he sought and that this would be revealed to him of itself when the time was right.

In 1925, aged 24, Bapak was out walking one night when a brilliant ball of light descended from the sky and entered his body, a light that lit up the whole countryside and was witnessed by many people in the locality. This light initiated a strong vibration within his being, a manifestation of the great life force which, years later, he was to speak of in the following terms:

> Now this vibration, this power we experience after the opening, is the vibration that exists within all things, within the whole universe: it is the basis or the beginning of the whole universe. In the Christian religion, this power or this vibration that we receive in the latihan is called the Holy Ghost.

When this power arose within him, Bapak's first thought was that he must be suffering a heart attack. He returned home and lay down, expecting to die. Instead, he was moved to stand up and pray.

Thus did Bapak receive the very first spiritual exercise of Subud—a special state that was to arise within him every night thereafter for the next three years. Throughout this time he hardly slept, although he continued to maintain a job and fulfill all other normal responsibilities of family and daily life.

During these years of continuous nightly latihan Bapak encountered an infinite variety of inner and outer experiences as an extraordinary process of spiritual transformation and realization unfolded within him. Eight years later—after a "spiritual ascension" that took him "through all the heavens"—it was made known to Bapak that it was his mission to transmit this inner contact to all who asked for it.

So began the spread of Subud, starting with those of Bapak's inner circle of friends and fellow seekers who wished to join him in following the latihan, and reaching many parts of Indonesia during the next twenty years.

Though Bapak's inner guidance had indicated that the time would come when he would travel the world on behalf of Subud, he was content to remain in Indonesia until 1957, when he accepted an invitation to visit London as the guest of a small group of Westerners, a few of whom had already been opened in Indonesia and Cyprus.

Shortly after his arrival in England he was invited to take up residence at Coombe Springs, the Surrey home of John Bennett, where his visit happened to coincide with an international Gurdjieff seminar. It was there that the latihan met with an immediate and enthusiastic response that sent scores of overseas visitors home to spread the contact. Many of these in their turn invited Bapak to visit their own countries, and his planned short visit to England developed into a world tour that lasted for fourteen months. Amid this flurry of activity and excitement, the latihan quickly spread throughout Europe and America.

Bapak's visit to the West in 1957 proved to be only the first of many. For the rest of his life he maintained a tireless commitment to a succession of world journeys, giving lengthy explanations about the latihan to the steadily growing international membership that exists today in more than seventy countries.

The tapes and transcripts of Bapak's talks over the years possess a radiant content and clarity, and project an authority and wisdom that bear eloquent witness to the source of his guidance. Inevitably, they also testify to the spiritual stature of Bapak himself, although he never claimed to be anything other than an ordinary man. It was this humility and down to earth quality that set Bapak apart from some of the more self-promoting "gurus" of recent decades. Always concerned with differentiating between the message and the messenger, he consistently emphasized the importance of following the latihan and surrendering only to God.

Although increasingly in his later years Bapak encouraged people to write about their experiences, he did not believe that Subud should be promoted or publicized. "Subud should grow by example, not by advertising," he said. Since the early sixties, the association has, therefore, grown almost solely on the basis of word of mouth, and by the evidence of positive changes in the lives of those who have received the contact.

When Bapak died there were Subud groups scattered throughout the world, with a total active association of approximately 10,000 otherwise "ordinary" people whose only apparent common denominator is the fact that they have received and follow the latihan. Many of them never got to see or hear Bapak for themselves.

※　※　※

Today there are Subud groups in or near most major Western cities. Most groups remain quite small, but all include members well established in the latihan. It is the duty of some of these experienced men and women, known as *helpers*, to serve as witnesses in assisting newcomers to receive the same direct contact with the power of God that Bapak himself first received.

All that is required for this *opening*—and the consequent awakening of the soul (usually referred to in Subud as the *inner self*)—to be effected is for the applicant to stand quietly with a feeling of patience and surrender in the presence of Subud members doing the latihan. Many new people are immediately aware that something special and unexpected has happened to them, although others have to wait some time before becoming able to feel the direct action of their own latihan.

Helpers also have a responsibility for passing on the clarifications given by Bapak during his lifetime. They will explain that the latihan works and progresses in a process that is unique to each individual and totally in harmony with his or her own nature and needs. It is unconfined by dogma and is free of hierarchical interpretation or authority. It is *real*: its effectiveness undiluted and undiminished by space or time; its endurance unaffected by Bapak's passing.

In addition to answering questions to the best of their ability in the light of Bapak's advice and their own inner indications, helpers also have a duty, where appropriate, to *test* with or for members as a means of helping them obtain clarity and direction in their daily lives. Testing is, once again, a rather inexact English translation for the practice of formulating specific questions and then seeking guidance via the latihan. Linguistically, Indonesian members do not attempt to differentiate between testing and the latihan experience itself; both are simply called *receiving*.

All we can bring to the latihan, advised Bapak, is an attitude of patience, sincerity, and surrender to the will of God. Only God himself can do the rest, which is nothing less than the initiation of a process of purification and spiritual development. This usually begins on the physical level, a stage many have experienced as a general improvement in health, sometimes accompanied by specific and occasionally quite dramatic cures. The latihan gradually penetrates to the deepest aspects of one's being, as the inner self is brought to life and grows to assume its rightful place. When this true self comes into its own, Bapak explained, it is able to regulate and be served by the lesser forces that help to make up our nature, rather than be ruled and often misled by them as before.

Bapak's term for the passions and desires that arise from the lower forces and work through our hearts and minds was the *nafsu*. But although it was convenient to speak of these ancillary forces as "lower" and "separate," Bapak said the deeper reality is that everything merges in a total oneness. He often reminded us that the lower forces of the material, vegetable, and animal levels, although sometimes seen as obstacles on the spiritual path, are actually essential for our physical existence. "Man remains man," Bapak said; the lower forces will always be part of our life in this world and should indeed be used for our benefit in this realm.

On the worldly level, Bapak never ceased to urge us to set up business enterprises, both as an expression of individuality and self-reliance and as commercial ventures in which Subud members could pool their expertise and learn to work together in harmony. He also encouraged us to identify and develop our true talent through following the latihan so that, ideally, the career we pursue, the work we do, would be in accordance with our own inner nature.

Through enterprises, said Bapak, Subud members would learn to be guided by God in their everyday life exactly as in the latihan itself. Thus they would take care of their two main areas of responsibility: on the one hand to worship God, and on the other to provide for their needs in this world.

It was Bapak's hope that the pursuit of enterprises would also enable Subud members to contribute toward the creation of welfare projects for the benefit of the weak and needy in society at large "without distinction as to nation, social level, or situation." Much is already being achieved in this direction. At the time of this writing, Subud members are responsible for a wide range of social and welfare projects in over fifteen countries around the world. This work is carried out under the auspices of the Susila Dharma International Association, a Subud network officially affiliated to ECOSOC, the social arm of the U.N. In most cases these endeavors began as the fruit of an individual's inspiration or inner guidance.

Bapak sometimes compared the inner awakening set in motion by the latihan to the opening and blossoming of a flower, a process that progresses of itself and in its own season. He warned against wishing to copy someone else, to be like anyone else. "You will become you from head to toe," he said. "You will be complete." He also explained that, because of the spiritual connection from generation to generation, the action of the latihan within us would also benefit, cleanse, and lift up our forebears, suggestive of an inner reversal of the "sins of the fathers" being visited upon their descendants.

The path of purification and growth can at times be painful, especially as one is made all too aware of one's own particular faults and failings, and is required to let go of limited ideas of one's true identity. In extreme cases this process may lead to a state of crisis, a period of intense purification when deep, fundamental aspects of a person's nature are exposed and worked upon by the latihan. The form this spiritual transition will take varies from person to person and reflects the individual's character. A quiet, self-contained person does not necessarily evince anything untoward in his or her conduct, while for others the experience may manifest in erratic behavior. Some may exhibit all the symptoms normally associated with a nervous breakdown.

An all-out Subud crisis is in fact relatively rare; it is by no means necessary for everyone to have one! The likelihood of doing so can in fact be lessened by adhering to Bapak's advice not to overindulge in the latihan, not to try and "go faster than God." Nevertheless, he also said that, although a crisis may be considered undesirable, someone who was obliged to undergo the experience would afterwards be glad of it.

It is no more possible to adequately describe the latihan itself to anyone who has not experienced it than to anticipate what any given man or woman will encounter in his or her own exercise. This will depend entirely on the nature of each individual and is an exclusively personal experience for everyone.

For each half-hour latihan the domination of the emotions and thinking (heart and mind) is to an increasing degree reduced by the power of God. During the latihan period each person freely follows whatever impulse (sound, movement, etc.) may arise from within. As the process and its accompanying awareness progresses, one is trained more and more to move and act from the inner self. In this way one gradually becomes accustomed to recognizing and feeling the difference between this guided state and the "normal" condition of moving and acting under the influence of what should more appropriately be our subordinate powers.

A developing awareness of this kind of spiritual chemistry is the essence of the Subud experience. It is the automatic outcome of each person's receiving, a term used to describe both the content of the latihan itself as well as the inner guidance and indications that may manifest at other times.

At any one group latihan, therefore, people might be laughing, shouting, praying, chanting, crying, singing, kneeling, jumping, dancing, or indeed being absolutely still and quiet. If this sounds bizarre, so must in their time have seemed the behavior of David "dancing before the Lord with all his might," (2 Samuel) and the Pentecostal fervor of the first disciples (Acts). In the latihan, however, everyone is having his or her own unique experience, and they are rarely distracted by what is happening around them. As Bapak said, "It may seem strange, but it's real."

Men and women exercise separately, and at first members limit their latihan to two sessions a week with the local group. Later, when accustomed to the experience, it may be appropriate to add a third latihan alone at home. In addition, most people find that the latihan arises spontaneously within them from time to time, an occurrence that becomes increasingly frequent as their growth progresses. In fact, Bapak would say that if we truly surrender to God, we will be aware of the presence of the latihan in the midst of *whatever* we do, a Subud equivalent of what many Christians would call, "prayer without ceasing."

He expressed this ideal in very poetic terms in August 1986:

> It is important to stay in touch with the latihan.
> To feel the vibration when you get up in the morning…
> to remember to feel for the vibration when you are
> in the middle of working…to bless your food at lunch and
> allow the latihan to rinse out your activities. During the
> afternoon, feel the vibration once or twice. At supper,
> bless your food and get quiet. Don't wait for Wednesday
> night or Sunday night to surrender. God has given you the
> chance to live near him day by day: don't relegate him
> to once or twice a week.

All we can do from the outer point of view to aid the inner self in its process of liberation and purification, counseled Bapak, is to practice self-denial whenever it may feel necessary. This can take the form of occasional fasting or cutting back on sleep or on other habits and pleasures. Such a discipline can be dedicated to attaining outer needs and goals as well as to nourishing inner patience and quiet.

Bapak also attached great importance to observing an annual month-long fast, such as the Lent of Christianity or the Ramadan of Islam. These are actually identical in essence, value, and intent, he said, and represent the only thing a human being can actively do to "help" almighty God. He went so far as to say that, health permitting, the yearly fast is essential for anyone who is serious about the spiritual life. It is equivalent, he once said, to doing the latihan for three years.

For many in both East and West, the keeping of this traditional holy month of fasting has degenerated into a somewhat empty ritual. But, Bapak explained, the weakening effect of the outer observances should, more importantly, serve to facilitate the *true* fast, namely: the *inner* abstinence from ungodly thoughts, feelings, desires, and actions.

It may well seem strange that so many non-Muslim Subud members are in the habit of keeping Ramadan. For many this is undoubtedly because it felt especially significant to be able to fast at the same time as Bapak himself for so many years. But it might also well be that Ramadan is perceived as offering a more structured, well-defined procedure than the rather vague, diluted Western approach to Lent. The discipline of Ramadan calls for thirty days of abstinence from food, drink, smoking, and sex between sunrise and sunset, although Bapak suggested that the latter prohibition be a full month-long denial. These outer observances, he explained, should be coupled with self-awareness and self-restraint in terms of behavior, thoughts, and attitudes.

Bapak spoke at length and in great detail about the meaning and importance of the fast, and many Subud members have come to recognize the value and benefit of following his advice in this connection. As a result, they have discovered within themselves a precious interior world of serenity and detachment. Each holy month becomes a process in its own right, not unlike the latihan itself. It is again unique to each person, an act of *willingness* rather than an act of *will*.

Bapak consistently emphasized that Subud is not a religion. The latihan, he often said, has come at a time when men and women demand proof—not words; a time when mankind in general finds it difficult to sustain a simple faith in God based purely upon the teaching and advice contained in the great religions. Furthermore, many people today consider a specific religion to be too restrictive, although Bapak felt that Subud members who do adhere to a particular religion should remain true to their own faith. He described the latihan nonsecularly as the spiritual reality—the *inner truth*—that lies at the heart of all the great religions and for which seekers in every age have yearned. The latihan, said Bapak, has the power to restore life and understanding to religion. Many Subud people of vastly diverse beliefs bear witness to the truth of Bapak's words, testifying that the latihan has brought them back to their own religion, their faith clarified and strengthened.

It was Bapak's contention that such immediate access to almighty God was generally made available through a succession of chosen messengers. With the latihan, he explained, God involves himself *directly* in the affairs of all those who receive it, making his power and guidance freely available to ordinary men and women who sincerely wish for this contact in the midst of their everyday lives. This dispensation, he said, is a timely intervention that has come about in our era precisely because the increasingly powerful influence of the material life force now seriously threatens the peace and very survival of the world.

Bapak's repeated assertion that Subud is not a religion is borne out in the multireligious character of the association itself. Subud groups include members from every major faith, all doing the latihan together without any of the usual sectarian conflicts. Nowhere is this affirmation of the intrinsic oneness of the human race and, therefore, real hope for future peace and harmony on earth more in evidence than at a Subud world congress. At these gatherings, people of all creeds and colors and from all walks of life find themselves united, enveloped, and guided by the spiritual exercise of Subud.

Such a spontaneous unification of rich and poor, of Muslim, Jew, Christian, Buddhist, and Hindu, as well as of those who would profess no particular religion, demonstrates that a direct personal contact with the divine source is now available to all people everywhere, regardless of race and religion—to all those who can feel the truth present in these words.

A Spiritual Apprenticeship

Coombe Springs in the late fifties had to be the spiritual hub of the universe, or so it seemed: an instant Mecca miraculously transported to one of the greenest and most pleasant parts of England's green and pleasant land. Every night scores of eager new Subud members from far and wide made their way to Coombe to take their places in the round of latihans that kept the place throbbing late into the evening.

My own twice weekly visits were easily the high spots of a life made suddenly rich and meaningful. In finding Subud I knew that I had come home. I was discovering that the kingdom of heaven really was within me. Gone was the earnest scanning of library shelves and the mental harvesting of theories and philosophies. I knew that the *reality* of the latihan was what I had been searching for all along.

Every latihan was an adventure—a magical mystery tour of sound and movement, as this miraculous contact spread its inner wings and led me, often quite literally, on a merry dance of self-discovery. Simultaneously both relaxing and exhilarating, each latihan was, superficially, a marvelous release from the tensions and pressures of the moment. More deeply, I knew that I was participating in one of the marvels of this or any other age: an awesome dispensation of grace and revelation comparable to any in history.

Subud, it was becoming increasingly clear, was a spiritual bonanza in which, through the power of God alone, we were brought to the feet of the Most High in the purest form of worship imaginable.

I had been opened exactly one month after getting married. Although Suzanna had never been a spiritual seeker, she was soon influenced by my enthusiasm and three months later she, too, came to Subud.

Within a few months local groups began to form wherever there were enough people in a neighborhood. I was among the dozen or so founding members of the Northwood group, just north of London. This was later to develop into the Loudwater group, still thriving today at Loudwater Farm, Rickmansworth, Hertfordshire.

The comparatively rapid growth of Subud and the proliferation of small groups in the U.K. at that time created a pressing need for local helpers to look after new members, and I was one of many youthful and inexperienced people pressed into service to meet the emergency.

After I had blithely followed the latihan for a couple of years, a period which in retrospect could perhaps be described as something of a spiritual honeymoon, its action began to reach in more deeply, cutting through my self-deception. I began to be painfully aware of some of the less savory aspects of my nature: cowardice, lust, impatience, and jealousy prominent among them.

Today I believe that becoming conscious of and dealing with the negative side of our being may well have been what Jesus had in mind when he said, "Take up your cross and follow me." Then, however, instead of accepting the experience as necessary to gain insight into my own nature, I regarded this growing awareness with a sense of shame and self-reproach.

I was particularly troubled by the insecure aspects of my character. I found myself undergoing an emotional crisis, in which I experienced unexplained states of general anxiety and intense fear. There was a two-week period in which I fully expected to die at any moment. I didn't know what was happening to me, but it was terrifying, the more so because I could find no external cause for my distress.

In my confusion I wrote to Bapak for clarification, and Sudarto, one of the longest-established Indonesian helpers, replied that their testing and receiving indicated that something had happened to me as a child to make me afraid of death. I was experiencing such fear and anxiety now because the latihan had begun to expose the injured aspects of my heart to the healing light.

His words evoked a vivid memory of how, as a child of about five years old in World War Two, our locality had been devastated in a bombing raid and I had been carried through burning streets to safety. A stick of bombs had fallen within fifty yards of our house, killing and injuring neighbors, and we had been showered with broken glass and other debris from the blast. "Please, can I go to Heaven now?" I had asked my mother, scared of being blown to pieces at any moment.

But there was nothing to worry about, Sudarto reassured me: "Your inner self is quite powerful enough to subdue your nafsu. It is only necessary to surrender everything to the power of God." Just trust in God, he wrote, "and all anxiety will disappear from your heart."

There was also a message from Bapak. "Sometimes God allows those with a strong heart to experience the crisis state so as to enable them to know the true situation," he said.

Soon after this, the ailing characteristics of my "strong heart" were shown to me in a dream. In the dream I was obliged to share a room with an old man, who was the embodiment of sorrow and self-pity, blindly blundering in all directions. He was immensely powerful, with muscles of iron. No amount of struggle on my part could evict him, and this insight helped me to understand Bapak's words. "Knowing the true situation," I realized, referred to a need to recognize and differentiate between my false identity and my real self. I saw that I could not evict the strong old man, who at that time was such an entrenched aspect of my own nature. Instead, I had to learn to live with him, to be at peace with him, without allowing him to run my life in his blind and blundering way.

At that time I was twenty-four years old, still in the R.A.F. and by now a member of the intelligence staff at the British Embassy in Washington, D.C., liaising with the Pentagon. I had come to hate Service life and was becoming increasingly depressed and frustrated with my meaningless role in the Cold War machine. And though I had several years still to serve, I nevertheless longed to be free to pursue activities more in keeping with my true temperament. My wish was about to be granted in a way I hadn't bargained for.

One day in the office, quite out of the blue, I was suddenly overwhelmed by the futility of my outer life and work. To my horror, I buried my face in my hands in full view of my colleagues and burst into tears. There had been no particular provocation or buildup of tension that I was aware of; it was as if a mask had been gently but firmly removed to reveal the true feelings beneath. It was a strange and distinctly uncomfortable experience! Unsure how to react to what might well be construed as a threat to the highly sensitive material I handled, the authorities arranged for my immediate return to England. Within a month I was a civilian.

My wife's reaction to this situation says a great deal about her character and inner strength. Although by now we had two small children, and despite the fact that Suzanna was really enjoying her life in America, she accepted the upheaval calmly and without complaint. Her support for me in my time of need was absolute.

As for me, alarmed at what had happened and dismayed at my seemingly infinite array of character defects, I began to develop a very ambivalent love/hate relationship with the latihan that persisted for the next two years. I was just too involved to be able to recognize that the purifying action of the latihan was at work, causing my long-buried problem areas to rise to the surface and be healed. Instead of relaxing, trusting God and going with the process, therefore, I started to become afraid of the latihan and blamed it for my own inner discord. I took my hand from the plough, in other words, and looked back.

My state at that time was conveyed in what turned out to be a very precognitive dream, in which I was climbing up a very steep hill.

Although the way ahead was smooth and not really difficult to climb, the summit was still a long way off, and I had only ascended about a tenth of the way when I looked down. At once my head swam and I lost my balance, whereupon a voice said, "Imagine falling from the top." I knew that "the top" signified the completion of an important stage of the purification or preparation phase of my Subud process, and that a condition of trust and surrender would always be necessary along the way.

Later in my journey I was to be glad of this early lesson. Like St. Peter, who—however metaphorically—sank beneath the waves when he temporarily lost faith in his capacity to walk on water, I had learned the hard way that it was vital to keep to the path I had chosen.

There would be no turning back.

Inner Guidance

S o many and varied are the ways people in Subud receive inner guidance and personal revelation that I often equate these spiritual fruits of the latihan with the prophecy of Joel: "And it shall come to pass after this, that I will pour out my spirit upon all flesh; and your sons and your daughters shall prophesy, your old men shall dream dreams, your young men shall see visions." (Joel 2:28)

There are of course many other Biblical references to the spiritual significance of inspired dreams, in particular, as a source of guidance and revelation. And the Prophet Muhammad, the founder of Islam, spoke of the inward signs he received at the beginning of his mission as "true visions" that came to him in his sleep.

For me, and for many other Subud people as well, a certain kind of clear dream has become an increasingly meaningful way of receiving inner indications and guidance other than during the latihan itself.

Bapak recognized that many dreams are only a projection of a person's ideas and imagination, and that clear receiving dreams are rarely experienced by people whose hearts and minds are still full of thoughts and emotions. Referring to spiritually significant dreams in Tokyo in 1967, he said that sometimes "people have a dream which in its nature is an indication of what is going to happen. It then turns out that what they have received in their dream really comes true."

I can only say that throughout much of my thirty-three years of following the latihan, it has been quite commonplace for me to receive invaluable counsel in the form of dreams; to be shown in dreams the reality of my own state and that of other people and situations; and to dream of future events either just before or sometimes long before they occur. In fact, I have been blessed with so much convincing personal experience of inner guidance manifesting through dreams that I have come to take the phenomenon somewhat for granted.

Much later in my Subud life guidance began to manifest itself in the form of visions, but from relatively early on indications arose in the form of insight or intuitive knowledge, or as a spontaneous awareness of another's state. A typical, if uncomfortable, instance of the latter occurred when I opened a colleague's door, stepped into his office, and almost doubled over with a sudden, sharp pain in my abdomen. "That's funny," he said, "I've been having excruciating stomach pains all afternoon."

The functioning of this inner antenna is not always so seemingly pointless. On one occasion I was driving a car crowded with our young family when I suddenly realized that just ahead was a snarl-up caused by an ambulance that had been forced to a halt right across our path. I had been driving too fast and not paying full attention. It was too late to brake effectively and I could see no way through. A serious accident seemed inevitable, and my mind went blank. In that instant the latihan took over my whole being. I watched in amazement while my hands and feet came alive and juggled with steering wheel, brake, and gear change. I was astonished as, with unerring judgment and an extraordinary delicacy of touch, I piloted our hurtling vehicle through an unsuspected gap in the traffic with inches to spare. Except that "I" had nothing to do with it! Years later, I asked my eldest daughter if she remembered the incident. "How could I ever forget it?" she laughed. "I couldn't believe it when you just took your hands off the wheel!"

Examples of such interaction between the miraculous and the mundane are legion among Subud people: like the story of the train passenger who was suddenly impelled—for no discernible reason—to vacate her seat and move to the one behind her. Seconds later a rock crashed through the window exactly where she had previously been sitting. Although showered with splinters of glass, she was completely unharmed.

Receiving by way of an *inner voice* seems to be an increasingly common source of guidance for many Subud members long established in the latihan. This phenomenon has been a natural and integral part of my own life for so long that it is perhaps appropriate at this point to recount the striking circumstances in which my own inner voice first made itself heard.

At the time I was working as a herdsman on a dairy farm, taking something of a sabbatical from my usual more commercial pursuits. I looked after a Guernsey herd of about sixty milkers, and each day began with the chore of putting my charges through a 4 x 4 herringbone milking parlor. For the benefit of the uninitiated, a herringbone parlor accommodates an equal number of cows, in this case four, on each side of the herdsman, who works from a central well between them. This arrangement puts his head at the level of the upper part of the cow's legs and so allows him easy access to her udder.

Many herds have a percentage of troublemakers, who are of course well known to the herdsman. Toward these he will be especially cautious in view of his extreme vulnerability in the well of the parlor.

In this particular herd, however, there were few such problem cases, and certainly never among the first thirty or so animals. These would make their way eagerly into the parlor in almost the same order every day, relaxed and looking forward to a good feed.

One cow in particular, Dignity V, was typical of this easygoing category. On the day in question she was, as usual, in the first group to enter the parlor, second only to Rosina, the acknowledged leader of the herd.

All seemed normal, and I fed the first four prior to washing their udders, a far from delicate procedure if one was to remove the dirt and mud picked up from a night in the field. It was also the sort of task one tended to carry out on automatic pilot and, having attended to Rosina, I reached out casually toward Dignity.

My hand was within a few inches of her udder when a great voice echoed through the parlor, seemingly both within and outside of me: "Be careful of this one." Strangely, I didn't think to question the fact of the voice itself. All that registered was its strong, commanding quality.

I froze and took a hard look at Dignity. Seeing nothing wrong, I flattened myself against cow number three and, using her body as a shield, reached out and very gently touched one of Dignity's teats. She responded instantly with the most ferocious kick imaginable, cleaving the air in deadly fashion precisely where my head would have been but for the warning voice.

Subsequent examination revealed a horrible wound to the far side of the teat I had touched, an injury completely invisible from my position in the well of the parlor, and in a place that in the normal course of events I would have grasped with some vigor.

As it was, her response, even to the gentlest of touches, was such that I would never have survived that kick.

These days, although it is not always easy to speak of one's own experience in this regard, I will simply and sincerely say that my own inner voice arises constantly and spontaneously—encouraging, advising, warning, or simply praying.

Outer Endeavor

The farming diversion was but a brief interlude in a working life spent for the most part in a succession of business enterprises, always in a sales and marketing capacity. My abrupt departure from the R.A.F. had opened the door for the flowering of my real talent, and—my early brush with the "crisis state" behind me—it hadn't taken me long after leaving the Air Force to gravitate toward selling I even spent a couple of early years as a door-to-door salesman, flourishing amid the challenges and uncertainties of what many people would regard as a daunting way of life.

Although I always worked very hard, I also surrendered the outcome of each day to God, never pushing too hard for business but confident that my efforts would always meet with a sufficient reward. I remember one puzzled housewife trying to express her feeling that surely I was not really a salesman. "You are just too... human," she said.

I soon discovered that if I followed Bapak's advice and channeled my heart and mind toward the things of this world—instead of toward spiritual matters—then my latihan, left to itself, became much lighter and stronger, clearly benefiting from the noninterference of thoughts and feelings.

At around the age of thirty I began to take Bapak's guidance about standing on our own feet very much to heart. From then on I have always been self-employed.

I invariably chose tough start-up situations calling for a high degree of commitment. I seemed to need a very challenging lifestyle that made enormous demands upon my time and resources, leaving little left over for anything else.

Typical of these undertakings was an early venture into the wine business, challenge enough for a teetotaler who knew absolutely nothing about wine!

This opportunity presented itself during a rare period when I was without work, at a time when we were really up against things from a material standpoint. It had taken Suzanna and me only ten years to produce six marvelous children, and at this point we were all living in what can only be described as a Subud commune in Cheltenham, Gloucestershire. We had no home of our own, no car, very little money, and a flourishing brood of young children to provide for. Things looked so tough that I felt driven to apply for welfare assistance. Yet when the check arrived, I sent it back. In spite of the apparent hopelessness of our situation, I was reluctant to risk succumbing to dependence on anything other than myself and God. I recognized that a time of seemingly greatest difficulty could also be a time of greatest blessing and opportunity, demanding as it did a deeper and truer faith and trust than usual.

When the offer first came my way I turned it down. Klaus had heard about my sales attributes from a mutual friend, and telephoned from London to ask if I would like to set up a West Country extension of his new wine import business. I explained that I did not really see how, as a nondrinker, I could possibly fit into such a project, thanked him and said goodbye. Three weeks later, and down to our last £20, I felt that I could no longer afford such scruples. I called Klaus and became a wine merchant.

We handled a range of fine French and German wines, and I found it to be a fascinating field of study. I was a comparative newcomer to Cheltenham and knew no one outside the small Subud community, but, using the telephone, I set up wine tastings at homes and businesses all over town. Within a few months I had created a lucrative network of private customers to whom I would sell large consignments of quality wines by the case. The hardest part in the early days was to project a credible image when I didn't even know what the wines tasted like! I overcame this by listening carefully to the informed comments of my first customers as they tasted the wines, and then using these observations to introduce my products to others. In this way I soon acquired a totally unfounded reputation for being a wine expert! It was not until later, I have to confess, that I came to appreciate for myself the subtle delights upon which I had expounded.

Before long I was able to buy a shop with ample living accommodation, from which Suzanna ran a retail sales department while I continued to develop my direct supply customer base. Our next move was to lease a warehouse and begin servicing the local restaurant trade. By this time I was also travelling the country, training others in our modus operandi and helping to set up similar operations.

My motto had become, "Work as if it all depends on you; pray as if it all depends on God," and I was able to call upon great reserves of energy and enthusiasm. These assets, coupled with a talent for getting along with others, guaranteed a reasonable level of success, both during my six years in the wine trade and during an equally demanding five years I spent afterwards building up a direct sales cookware business.

My work often took me away from home. Later, although I loved my family very much, I wondered to what extent my over-involvement with business may have reflected an urge to be free of the confines and responsibilities of domesticity. I became increasingly aware of a vulnerability toward women.

For, despite my success, I felt somehow unfulfilled. I was often aware of a nagging loneliness—an indefinable sense of need and fear. I would combat this underlying insecurity by working even harder, by prayer, by conscious efforts at "positive thinking" and, most effectively, by way of regular fasting on Mondays and Thursdays.

And, of course, the latihan was always there, helping to maintain an inner balance and serving to offset a workaholic tendency that otherwise might well have brought about my total absorption in the material world.

Observing the Ramadan fast had also become an increasingly valuable and meaningful way of maintaining that balance. Ramadan had become "the best month of the year," an annual inner sanctuary from outer activity and turbulence.

The Ramadan of 1982 was of particular importance for me, developing into something of a personal retreat after a grueling eleven years in the direct sales business. I welcomed the fast more than ever that year, sensing that my cookware business had run its course and that it was time to move on. Although normally I continued to work during Ramadan, this time I resolved to let go completely, confident that a new direction would open up for me.

"When one door closes another opens" was one of my mother's favorite expressions. The maxim certainly held true at the end of that Ramadan, when Andrew Bromley offered me a partnership in a printing company he had started a few years earlier. The business was doing fine but was still quite small and needed a sales boost. Andrew was a fellow member of the Loudwater Subud group, and an old friend of many years. The offer was right up my street.

We prospered, and within a year we had launched another enterprise—an advertising and marketing agency—in partnership with designer Marcus Bolt, another old friend. Before long we had set up a third venture—a typesetting company—joined by yet another Subud friend, Leonard Hurd, with whom I had shared a great deal over the years. To house our growing group of companies we bought a medium-sized commercial building.

My own role still encompassed the generation of new business, but a flair for copywriting and the more creative aspects of marketing had emerged, and these aspects began to make more and more demands on my time. We were all working very hard, long hours, and even Sundays were usually given over to brainstorming our clients' advertising campaigns.

By the mid-eighties we were making a good living from our Subud enterprises, and we were also able to contribute financial support to the association itself as well as to a few charities, both Subud and others. Moreover, the experience of working closely with other Subud members, all subject to our respective purification processes, added a valuable new dimension that was sometimes beautiful, sometimes difficult, but always enriching.

But if it was clear that I was capable of going places in the material world, it soon became equally apparent that, in the process, I had left my emotional life just as far behind. Having successfully suppressed my most troubling emotions for so long by submerging myself in work, perhaps I should not have been surprised to see them rise to the surface once, materially, I had nothing more to "go for."

It began at first in a very subtle way, as deep inside I could feel the ground of my being shifting within me. As time passed I became aware of an increasing sense of losing my way, if not my very identity. I buried myself even more deeply in my work, but I knew that the inner confrontation with the negative aspects of my character loomed large once more. It was as if the very forces that constituted my "strong heart" were threatening to erupt, and I felt as if I would explode under the pressure. This time, I sensed, I was heading for a momentous personal showdown that nothing would avert. It seemed as though my very selfhood was disintegrating. My life became a desperate struggle to conceal the chaos within and present a credible front to the world, to family, colleagues, and clients alike.

It was around this time, again during the month of Ramadan, that I had a vision of great significance. The inner self of Marianne, a dear Subud friend of many years, who at that moment lay stricken with cancer with only one week to live, appeared to me and said, "You will stay at the top till the very end." It was an unmistakable reference to the mountain climbing dream of so many years before, and clearly intended to give me courage and faith in the face of what lay ahead.

A Light from Space

A gainst this backdrop of personal trauma, my weakening marriage suffered a body blow.

Suzanna and I had married young, ages twenty and twenty-one, respectively. Perhaps, therefore, I felt I had missed out on early years of freedom or had chosen too soon. Notwithstanding her fine character and outstanding qualities as loyal wife and devoted mother, I often felt disappointed that Suzanna was not the obvious spiritual seeker I longed for in a partner. I yearned for union with the "perfect woman," a profoundly spiritual person who would also be capable of satisfying my passionate and sensual nature on every level. My heart and mind, those perpetual playgrounds of the nafsu (desires and passions), were, therefore, easily persuaded that our marriage was not "ideal."

Our relationship deteriorated markedly in the late seventies when I began to take a serious interest in Lucia [not her real name]. Lucia was in her early twenties, about half my age, and we had become good friends while working closely together in business. She was beautiful and spirited, a long way from her home overseas, and my initial affectionate concern for her well-being developed into love. Before long we had drifted into a full-blown affair despite inner indications to the contrary, which I allowed my "strong heart" to distort and overrule.

Soon I was in effect leading a double life, leaving home at 9 a.m., seeing as much as possible of Lucia throughout the day, and rarely getting home again before 11 p.m. This deceitful regime was facilitated by the fact that my business at that time required me to work most evenings.

Although I felt I wanted to marry Lucia, my youngest children were still only in their mid-teens and I could not contemplate leaving the family at that stage. Matters remained unresolved while Lucia went abroad for a couple of years. We remained in contact, and early in 1985 I broached the subject of separation with Suzanna. She was devastated, and, torn between the wishes of my heart and my horror of inflicting so much pain upon Suzanna, I dropped the subject and did my best to comfort her.

Six months later Lucia returned to England, and we made plans to get together. This time, unable to bear witnessing the suffering I knew

40

it would cause Suzanna, I wrote a letter of explanation and left without warning.

I had hoped this decisive action would help to reverse my process of inner disintegration. But in fact it only exacerbated my deterioration, and I moved through these events as if in a dream. I bought a small apartment for Lucia and myself in West London, but nothing seemed quite real.

In the past, I had usually been able to keep the more negative, insecure aspects of my nature under control through prayer and occasional fasting. Suddenly that was no longer possible. Indeed, the exact opposite became the case. The slightest expression on my part of a self-willed prayer or intent to fast, or indeed to initiate any hitherto positive action, now actually *incurred* the very states they were intended to subdue!

There ensued a nightmare beyond description, months in which the concept of *I* no longer had any meaning. *I* had become nothing more than a vortex of vicious, fearful forces.

This grim phase came to a head during the middle of a night in late October 1986, with what I was later able to identify as the first in a series of real—however remarkable—experiences that, from the point of view of the ordinary mind, I am quite unable to explain or understand.

I awoke to find myself in latihan. But I was not in bed. I was wide awake and standing on a hillside with two unidentified companions.

I looked up and watched with detached interest as a bright light like a shooting star, the most intensely bright light I had ever seen, arched through the sky from deep in space heading toward earth.

The whole episode felt quite natural, and at first I was not at all alarmed. But suddenly I knew that the light was in some way connected with myself, was in fact heading straight for me. I began to feel afraid.

In my panic I ran behind a nearby wall in the hope of hiding from the fast approaching light. Looking back, I saw that a satellite receiving dish had appeared on the very spot I had just vacated. The dish was so angled that when the light struck it, it ricocheted straight at me, still cowering behind the wall.

The light entered my body and, with one convulsive shudder, expelled the warring forces that had been making my life so miserable for so long. I "came to" in bed and fell instantly into a deep, relaxing sleep.

I awoke in the morning more at peace and at home within myself than I could ever remember feeling. Surely my ordeal was over?

It had in fact just begun.

CRISIS

F or three weeks or so after being pierced by the light from space, I was calm and unburdened. My latihan was light and relaxed and the unpleasant inner states did not return.

Yet outwardly I became aware of a mounting sense of lethargy and lack of direction. It was as if I had lost whatever motivating force had driven my life to date. This condition of disorientation came to a climax about a week later.

I was driving on the M1, one of England's busiest highways, when, without any cause I could identify, a combination of strange and disconcerting physical symptoms began to manifest themselves. My heart began to pound erratically, my head to swim, and my breathing took on a frenzied rhythm of its own over which I had no control.

Driving became very difficult and, fearing I might be experiencing a heart attack, I pulled over to the slow lane and barely managed to keep going until I reached the family home—only a few miles away—that I had left almost a year earlier. There my daughters took charge and got me to the local clinic where my breathing remained wildly irregular and I struggled to remain conscious. Suzanna rushed to join us in time to hear the doctor diagnose my condition as a panic attack. Several injections later, clutching a prescription for tranquilizers, I tottered "home," assisted by my anxious family.

Although Suzanna and I had not met for about a year—during which time she had begun to rebuild her life following the shock of my departure—she was totally supportive. At the risk of jeopardizing her new-found self-reliance she agreed that I should stay at the house for a few days while I recovered sufficiently to be able to return to my apartment. The "children"—Howard, Francisca, Andrew, Dani, Louise, and Ros—were now aged between twenty-one and thirty-one, and only Ros, the youngest, was still living at home.

The day after my unscheduled arrival at my former home, Suzanna drove me into the countryside, where we walked slowly along a riverbank. It was in the stillness of that natural setting that I heard my inner voice say, "Your wife is the one to look after you at this time." In this way, although I had not asked for it, the latihan provided the clearest possible guidance, even in those fraught circumstances. It is a measure of the degree to which my outer life was dominated by my passions that I chose to ignore it. Once again my "strong heart" had the last word. Within a few days I returned to Lucia in West London.

The next month or so was a period of limbo, dominated by feelings of weakness at all levels and by a total lack of self-confidence. This condition was probably sustained to some extent by the prescribed drug, and I was shown clearly in a dream that the full dose was harmful and should be reduced. I began, therefore, to cut back on the pills and within a few weeks was able to stop taking them altogether.

At this stage I was not able to be aware that my breakdown was an integral part of an unfolding spiritual process that would lead to my own inner truth. It was impossible for me to think straight, and I wondered whether the illness might be nothing more than the outcome of years of overwork, coupled with the stress of my unresolved life situation. Needless to say, these were very traumatic weeks for Lucia too.

By this time it was becoming very clear to both of us that we did not belong together. For my part, I recognized that I had allowed the strong animal aspect of my nature to usurp the human. In following my passions I had been blind to the true interests and will of my inner self. I received that this was why I was now brought so low, and feared that I might have been rejected completely by God as a punishment for my willfulness. This anxiety was at once laid to rest by my inner voice: "There is no question of that, although you must be very careful in the future."

A complete break seemed to be the only answer. Lucia moved out, and I remained alone at the apartment, now—on top of everything else—battling also with a great sense of loss at parting from her,

Typically, I envisioned recovery as being synonymous with getting back on track in business, and in this vain pursuit I spent a ghastly few days at a so-called health farm, a highly prestigious establishment just outside London. There I was allocated a luxury room no doubt previously occupied by a succession of wealthy patrons recuperating from overexposure to the pressures of business and the excesses of the high life. Whatever the explanation, as soon as I lay down to sleep I was amazed to see droves of hideous, batlike creatures rise out of the bed, expelled by cleansing sheets of beautiful silver rain which fell around me. Strangely enough, I did not feel disturbed or frightened by the bats; I could only marvel at the grace and beauty of the rain from heaven.

I was grateful that my business partners, Marcus and Andrew, were also Subud brothers. They stood by me magnificently at a time when I felt as if I were hanging on to my sanity by a hairbreadth. They insisted I should feel no pressure about returning to the office. Their patience and forbearance were a lifeline, and they shared much of the trauma of those early weeks as well as many of the powerful latihans I was beginning to experience.

By now it was obvious that I was deeply in crisis, and during one rather desperate questioning and testing session I suddenly perceived that I was running around in circles looking for a way out; that I was actually hampering and delaying the smooth progress of whatever God willed for me. I saw, in short, that it was time to *surrender*.

This realization brought with it a glimmering of peace, and I cut short the testing with the certainty that I could now begin to leave the outcome completely in God's hands.

A few days later, alone in my apartment, I was suddenly possessed by a condition of personal annihilation, a state of total terror. It was so overwhelming, I felt I would not be able to prevent myself from rushing blindly into the street. But I knew there was nowhere to run. Perhaps I should telephone someone, anyone? But I also knew I would not be able to remember anyone's telephone number, let alone dial it.

Then: *No! This time, let me not run; let me experience all that this state has to offer; and let me not be afraid of the fear.* For the first time in many weeks, joy and hope began to whisper within me. From deep inside, the voice said, "Now you can begin to grow."

Facing my fear was a turning point in my journey to the light.

Complete Trust and Confidence

I t was as if my crisis proper could now proceed, and somehow it had to be a solitary affair. I still did not know who *I* was and relating to others was impossible. I felt transparent, defenseless, and acutely sensitive to what was going on in those around me. For weeks I isolated myself from virtually all contact, protected from the world by a new phone answering machine. I ventured out only on essential visits to the local shop and to attend group latihan.

I seemed to pass through a period of *deparenting*. I was given clear insight to view my parents in a very objective light as I relived childhood events and early conditioning. Inside myself I encountered previously repressed attitudes of resentment, frustration, and even hatred toward my parents. I had been an only child, sensitive and "highly strung," mirroring many of my parents' own characteristics. Now I realized that I had long blamed them for my own inadequacies. I had forgotten Bapak's advice that such an attitude was both inappropriate and unnecessary. It was only necessary, he said, to have faith in God and a feeling of trust in oneself— the true self that is a living individual in the womb before falling under parental influences.

Early on my mother had closed her mind against Subud, rejecting it as "non-Christian." This resulted in a tragic lack of true communication between the two of us that persisted for nearly thirty years, right up until a few days before her death. Outwardly, our contact had degenerated into a single weekly phone call, dutiful conversations without real content. Now I also realized how much I had missed sharing and expressing the spiritual bond between us that had been so evident in my childhood.

This was a very difficult time of black depression and pounding headaches, a sort of crash course in psychoanalysis but directed entirely from within by the latihan. In fact, I wondered whether I should seek professional psychiatric help, but testing showed this was not necessary. Deep down I knew that I was way beyond human help; that God himself was in charge and that I had no choice but to leave everything to him. Again and again the suffering and pressure would reach an unbearable level, and I would receive "rest awhile" or "enough for now." At the end of this phase I received, "You have already come a long way."

It was around this time that I spent three days in a state of desperate remorse for past errors and ways in which I had hurt others, especially Suzanna and Lucia. Weeping, I was driven to seek them both out and plead for forgiveness. In trying to communicate with Suzanna I was virtually incoherent with grief.

❀　❀　❀

Awareness and surrender became my watchwords as experience succeeded experience in what amounted to a virtual *reparenting* by the power of God. It was necessary for me to know and feel that I was truly a child of God, independent of all other creatures. During this time I found it necessary to spend at least six hours a day in latihan.

In fact, from this point life and latihan began to merge into one continuous flow, which has remained the case ever since. The latihan, I became increasingly aware, *is* life.

My experiences at this time were symbolized by a graphic dream in which I was brought before a court and accused of many offenses. Not only was I found not guilty of all charges, but the judge actually commended me on the *extent* of my innocence. Outside the court I was surrounded by journalists, all congratulating me on my acquittal and eager to report my story. I eluded them and lowered myself into an underground tunnel that led to an enormous skyscraper just a couple of blocks away. It was a post office depository, crammed with unclaimed letters and parcels. Turning to the reporters, I said, "Do you think I can let matters rest here when I've got *that* to go for?"

I felt sure that the "unclaimed mail" in the dream represented unrealized spiritual benefits of some kind: blessings, perhaps, I had missed out on through reacting against and, therefore, blocking my process in the early sixties. The same Sudarto who had written to me in those early days was later to elaborate on this interpretation during conversations in Jakarta, Indonesia, in 1989.

"You yourself are good," he said, "represented by being found innocent by the judge. The undelivered parcels symbolize the inherited impurities of your ancestors, which must also be purified." He pointed out that this very possibility, symbolized by my entry into the underground tunnel, was in itself a highly significant aspect of the experience. Clearly, I had a long way to go!

❀　❀　❀

Once my initial panic reaction subsided the intensive receiving continued for months on end. Now that I was able to go with the process rather than resist it, not a night would pass without one or more inner experiences of one kind or another, often quite startling. In one I received that I was undergoing a "crucifixion." In another I saw myself in a dream, calm, sitting upright and dressed in a smart business suit, being driven slowly to my own funeral. A large banner over the hearse bore the words, "Complete Trust and Confidence." In truth I often felt as if I had to face and accept death within myself in surrendering to whatever the night would bring, a necessity that helped to reinforce an attitude of total reliance upon God.

Such "clear dreams" became ever more commonplace. In addition to the more significant messages, most nights I would be shown edited highlights of the events of the next day, which always proved to be accurate down to the smallest detail.

My solitary suffering also continued, as I was led to let go of all previous interests, habits, and ways of being. For months this advertising copywriter, whose only spare time interests had been reading complicated espionage thrillers and watching comedy and drama on television, was quite unable to write even a postcard, to read as many as two words strung together, or to watch anything on TV!

I received that for me, work had in fact been "a substitute for being." Now I had no choice but to *endure* and to *be*, without a moment's escape into fantasy or relaxation.

I felt very much like a newborn child, vulnerable and unfamiliar with the world around me. In fact, I awoke from a doze one afternoon feeling exactly as if I had just been born, as if I had no past. Everything around me seemed so strange and new that I actually went from room to room as if looking at everything for the first time. I even went out in the car to see how the outside world looked. I was surprised that I still knew how to drive!

For a long time I continued to feel that I no longer had any basis for relating to anyone else on earth. I felt like an alien on this planet, a stranger among its inhabitants, incapable of relationship with anyone other than God. I began to understand what Jesus meant when he said, "The Son of Man hath nowhere to lay his head."

Signposts to Renewal

Overall, this period of intense suffering lasted about two years. During much of this time, fear and despair seemed to reign supreme within me, offering little hope that things would ever be different.

Early on in the process I was shown that my "learning curve" was necessarily long, gentle, and drawn out. I was also shown another's learning curve, and this was steep and comparatively short-lived. The reason for the difference, I was given to understand, was my lack of courage. My recovery was thus a long, slow process of learning to live and be all over again, albeit from an entirely different inner place.

Back in the early sixties, during my first taste of the "crisis state," I had had a very clear dream of a "before" and "after" nature that had a powerful effect upon me at that relatively early stage in my Subud life. It had come in two parts. In the first, I was on my knees before Bapak pleading for his help. I was devastated when he totally ignored me as if unable to acknowledge even the existence of a wretch such as I. In the second part, I was clearly much changed and chastened by the passage of time and deliberately remained at the back of a group crowding around Bapak, hoping he would not notice me. This time, however, he singled me out and put his arm around my shoulders. He flashed one of his glorious smiles and said, "Now you are one in heart with Bapak."

I knew that I had somehow been able to avoid this full crisis of purification back then. Now, some twenty-eight years later, with no choice but to go through it, I experienced a whole series of "before" and "after" dreams and visions.

In one, a dream, I had taken my car in for service. It was supposed to be a routine job, and I called to pick it up at the end of the day. It was not there with the other vehicles, however, and eventually I found it abandoned on rough ground behind the garage.

A mechanic came up, shaking his head doubtfully, and began to point out all sorts of defects of which I had been unaware. "You do realize that this car can't last much longer," he said. "No more than a couple of weeks."

"It doesn't matter," I replied lightly. "I'm getting my new one soon."

A week or so later, in latihan, I saw myself out on a hillside with two companions. We looked skyward and saw a brand-new car descending steadily through space. At once my companions began to fit me with a parachute so that I could leap off the earth and glide into the driver's seat as the car floated down.

On another occasion I saw myself in a waking vision encased in a thick mummylike outer shell made of lead, a chrysalis-like replica of my whole body. The top had begun to break away, exposing part of my real head.

A week or so later, I again saw myself inside an outer skin, also an exact replica, but now it was made of fine porcelain. It was broken away to below my knees, and it would have been a simple matter to step out of it altogether. These two experiences seemed graphically symbolic of the weakening and falling away of the negative aspects of my former self. I remembered one of Bapak's early remarks: "Sometimes when the plant grows the pot breaks."

Toward the end of January 1987, a couple of months after my collapse and well before the discernible beginning of a change for the better, I heard a commanding voice in the night saying, "*He* will come on the 16th." Three weeks later, at exactly 8 p.m. on February 16, I was pulled to my feet by the sudden charge of a very powerful vibration in both arms, for all the world as though both hands were plugged into high-voltage electricity.

I felt quite frightened, as for about fifteen minutes my arms and hands remained rigid, shaking in the grip of this immense power, before the experience settled down into a more normal latihan. Afterwards I received that this happening was a manifestation of a new and *personal* relationship with God.

This was one of the first indications I had that something was taking place other than a process of breakdown, but it was not until I had travelled much further along the road that I came to recognize how significant it was that this particular experience, with its suggestion of spiritual rebirth, had occurred on the 16th. The 16th, albeit of a different month, happens to be my birthday.

Some subsequent experiences, though not always so portentous, simply served to encourage me.

In one, I saw myself in a vision joined by a long silver cord to a much larger and brighter version of myself looking down from above. Then I was the bigger me, smiling down encouragingly at my smaller, ordinary self. I alternated between the two for a while, feeling equally at home as either. At the time it was a great comfort to be granted this vision of my strong, bright, higher self, so obviously able to guide and support the ordinary me during my ordeal.

In another, I saw myself in a dream walking shoulder to shoulder with a rugged, powerful man in his early sixties. "Do you know who this is?" asked a voice. "No," I replied. "That is a pity," the voice continued, "because this is one of the most caring people ever to walk on earth."

Not long afterwards I was again visited by the powerful charge of "high-voltage electricity," a much stronger version of the fine vibration sometimes felt during the latihan. I was then aware of all desire being expelled from my being, an experience that left me feeling extremely weak and vulnerable for several hours. Later that day, though, I felt uplifted and cleansed, and in that new clarity knew that the only meaningful future work for me would be somehow connected with Subud.

That night I had a particularly vivid dream, in which I had flown to Jakarta to be greeted very warmly and intimately by Bapak. He chatted lightly for a while and thanked me for my help. Then he reached out to shake my hand in farewell. Still holding my hand and with his feet still on the earth, his body stretched way up into the sky and his head disappeared into space.

From this point on, my experiences seemed increasingly to suggest that I would one day be guided to serve some higher purpose, none more vividly than the vision that followed a dream in which a radiant and dynamic Bapak came to comfort and advise me. He was wearing a bejewelled cloak and a golden headdress. A week later, while sitting quietly alone one Saturday afternoon in a quiet, relaxed state, I was suddenly showered from above with jewels, falling softly into place over my shoulders like multicolored flower petals to form a cloak. Upon my head descended an ornate headdress. I immediately recognized the cloak and crown as those worn by Bapak in my dream. I looked up, and above my head I saw a knight in full armor astride a magnificent charger.

Sudarto smiled broadly when I told him about this experience. "This means that you have been given a mission by Bapak," he said. "It reminds me of when Bapak used to go off on his travels around the world and leave me in a position of responsibility here in Jakarta. I would wonder how I could possibly fill such a role in his absence. Then I would see myself dressed in a sort of uniform given to me by Bapak and I would know that everything would be alright." He paused. "Your vision of the knight in armor is telling you the same thing: that you will always be given the power to carry through whatever will be required of you."

The Heart Transplant

On March 25, 1987, I received the most powerful of all the crisis latihans. It started as a dream but immediately developed into a waking experience.

In the initial dream sequence I found myself in an operating room used for heart transplant operations. Two surgeons entered, and to my horror I realized that I had been cast in the role of patient. I protested vigorously that it must be a mistake, but the surgeons ignored my pleas and prepared to operate. One had a very long strip of adhesive tape across his own chest on the outside of his rubber gown, and I knew this meant that he himself had once been the subject of just such an operation. Both took great interest in inspecting the surgical instruments, and one said to the other, "I wonder whether they still do things the way we used to in our day."

At this point I awoke and was able to see right up into the night sky, the walls and roof of my bedroom having completely disappeared. I saw two angels descending to earth carrying between them an enormous heart, complete with trailing arteries. The organ itself was about two-thirds as big as the angels. And it was transparent; I could see right through it to the stars beyond. I wondered what it could be made of, and a voice answered "Diamond."

I closed my eyes and soon felt the onset of a very powerful vibration in my chest, yet another charge of "high-voltage electricity." I felt afraid and was sure I must be dying from a heart attack. But—because I was quite alone and knew there was absolutely nothing I could do about the situation—I was able to relax my body and surrender everything to God.

For some time in latihan I had been receiving a progressive state of surrender to what I can only call the attributes of God: "I surrender to the grace, majesty, wisdom, and perfection of the one almighty God; I surrender to the will, purpose, and magnificence of the one almighty God; I surrender to the joy, happiness, and beauty of the one almighty God"; and so on, demonstrating, I felt, that all things truly good and noble can only come from him. I was now aware of these attributes flowing into my chest.

After a while the vibration stopped and I lay still, feeling as weak as I could imagine anyone feeling while still alive. Then I found myself looking down on my body lying on the bed, clothed like a knight crusader in a white tunic bearing the red cross of St. George.

Next, despite my weakness, I was compelled to get out of bed and was somehow "walked" into the next room. There I was made to kneel and prostrate myself in prayer before being returned to bed. Before falling asleep, I saw in the darkness above me a knight in armor, astride a magnificent horse.

"Did things begin to improve for you after this experience?" asked Sudarto during our talks in Jakarta two years later.

"Yes," I replied. "That's exactly what happened."

Ave Maria

A few days after the "heart transplant," I received, "It is now God's will that you become well and strong by being peaceful and quiet."

And later that same day, quite unexpectedly, I received, "Maria will lead you on. She will guide and strengthen you." From that time on the feeling of a growing relationship with Our Lady, the mother of Christ, became an increasingly significant aspect of my latihan. At other times too I was aware of her nearness and guidance. Her name would constantly arise within me.

Bapak always attached great importance to a person's name, maintaining that it should reflect inner reality. It had, therefore, long been the practice for Subud members to ask him for their "right" name, a responsibility and capacity that passed to Ibu Rahayu, Bapak's eldest daughter, in the year before his death.

Around this time, therefore, aware that I was undergoing a process of great change, I wrote to Bapak and asked for a new name. The reply, which came from Ibu Rahayu, was Marius, the masculine form of "Maria." It was wonderful to have this precious link reinforced in this way. Much later I visited the scenes of Our Lady's apparitions at Fatima, Portugal, and Guadaloupe, Mexico, and in both places this inner connection was reaffirmed in strong and beautiful latihans.

Yet, not long after receiving my new name, while going about my everyday life, I suddenly heard Bapak's voice loud and clear in my ear saying, "Then, I will tell you your *real* name." From that moment on, although I loved the name Marius and would have been happy to bear it forever, I knew that one day it would change. I began to feel that somehow it was a temporary support, an outward expression of Our Lady's inner help during the time of my extreme weakness.

My own family had long had good reason to recognize and revere the person of Mary.

Fifty years ago my father was seriously ill with tuberculosis, a killer disease in those days. Major surgery seemed inevitable, and a successful outcome was by no means certain. My mother, a devout Anglican Christian, had heard of the Shrine of Our Lady at Walsingham, Norfolk. It was known as a place of pilgrimage and healing, often referred to as "the Lourdes of England," and sometimes as "Little Nazareth."

It is recorded that in the year 1061 Mary appeared to Richeldis, the lady of the manor, and asked that a church be built in her name at Walsingham, close to a stream of pure water. This was duly accomplished, and Walsingham became the focus of centuries of worship and intercession.

To make the journey from our home in Devon in Southwest England to Norfolk was no small matter for my parents. Dad was weak from his long illness, and the family was very poor. We could afford to have chicken just once a year as a real treat, for example, which, needless to say, was on Christmas Day! Mum was determined, however, and somehow they managed to make the trip after weeks of prayer and preparation.

When they finally reached the tiny Norfolk village, they both were immediately absorbed into the serenity that pervades the area, which for most visitors is a sufficient blessing in itself. Nowhere is this concentration of peace and spirituality more palpable than in the Holy House, the inner sanctum of the Shrine of Our Lady. There, after drinking from the well, my parents knelt together in prayer. Neither could speak at this time. It was only later, sitting together in the tranquillity of the adjacent garden, that they realized they had both undergone an identical experience at the altar. Both had been aware of a sensation of dizziness, accompanied by what each described as "a sort of shivery feeling," an expression I was occasionally to hear used in later years to describe the latihan.

After a week's stay in Walsingham they returned home, and Dad kept an appointment for further X-rays and other medical examinations prior to readmittance to the hospital. To the amazement of the doctors, his lungs were now clear and it was quite unnecessary for him to have surgery.

Furthermore, although my mother had had only my father's recovery at heart in planning the pilgrimage, she herself had been a long time victim of diabetes. And her doctor was also in for a surprise when she, too, was discovered completely free of her illness. She was immediately able to discontinue all further treatment for the disease for the rest of her life.

From that time on Walsingham occupied a central place in my mother's devotional life, and occasional visits to the village were highlights of the remainder of her days. She often said that, for her, it represented the nearest thing to heaven on earth.

She died very suddenly in 1987 at age seventy-seven, in peace and contentment, keenly looking forward to yet another visit to Walsingham which we had been planning as a special treat for her just a few days later.

Without knowing it I had been prepared for her death in a dream two months earlier. In the dream I was walking beside a high wall along a tree-lined road with someone whose face I could not quite see. Suddenly this unidentified person turned to me and said, "There's nothing to it. By the time I hit the ground it will be over." In the event, the road on which Mum was to collapse and die so suddenly a few weeks later proved to be the one I had seen in my dream. And when I spoke to the hospital nurse, she said, "It might be of some comfort to know that your mother would not have suffered at all."

By an extraordinary "coincidence" a feeling of deep inner connection was reestablished between Mum and me in the few days before her death. Whereas our weekly contact had long been limited to one rather tense phone call, for some reason I was moved to phone her on each of the four days immediately prior to her death. Our conversations became progressively lighter, and during one of these calls I played her a short extract from a new compact disc I had bought especially for her to listen to while staying with us after the projected trip to Walsingham. It was Handel's Messiah, her all-time favorite, which I had also come to love as a child. I turned up the volume and held the phone away from me so that she could hear the music. When I moved the receiver back to my ear, it was to hear her voice soaring with the glorious strains of the orchestra. In that same instant I felt joined to her by the latihan in a deep thrill of joy and reconciliation.

That night I experienced a very strong dream latihan in which, imbued with great spiritual power and wielding a mighty sword, I was cleansing the Shrine at Walsingham as if in preparation for an event of significance. This is the only dream that I have ever had concerning Walsingham, and I did not receive any indication as to its meaning. But forty-eight hours later my mother was dead, and a week later I had a vision of her walking in the gardens of the Shrine of her beloved Lady.

My own feeling of the nearness of Mary continued to deepen. I revisited Walsingham and walked alone through the village my mother had loved so much. In the Shrine I experienced the oneness between my latihan and the spirituality of Mary, and I received that Mary is "the Queen of all nations."

I also received, "He has built within you a cradle for his love," beautiful words I was to have good cause to remember in October 1989 when I visited Medugorje, Yugoslavia, scene of Our Lady's most recent and frequent apparitions.

You Will Become Strong

I t was at this time that many of my inner experiences began to take me into space. The first of these happened one Sunday morning when, feeling a little weak and disoriented, I had gone to lie down. Suddenly I found myself high above the earth, looking down on the hazy beauty of the curve of its horizon far below. I looked up and a slit appeared in what I knew was the outer perimeter of this material world, through which I would pass if it were time. I might have expected such an astounding, wide-awake experience to be disturbing and frightening, but it was its natural quality that was so significant. I felt so free, light, and at home up there. It was returning to my body afterwards that felt awkward and alien.

I came to welcome the feeling of effortless travel beyond the confines of this world, where I began to feel increasingly secure and at home. Once I saw myself in orbit around the earth exactly like a satellite. The satellite was not yet operational, however; it was nonfunctional, as if waiting for mission control to throw a switch.

In the middle of the night of April 2, 1987, I found myself instantly wide awake and aware that something important was about to happen. A commanding voice announced, "Prophet Muhammad," and, although I couldn't see anyone, I was at once aware of his presence in the room.

Without any preliminaries we left this world and travelled deep into space, on and on. Although the distance involved was vast by earthly standards, somehow the journey did not take long. I was fully conscious and was aware of a faint whooshing sound. Eventually we came to a halt and stood together gazing at an enormous edifice, majestic and inpenetrable, still farther out in space. I was not told what it was. After a while I said in awe, "No one can look at this for too long," and we turned back.

During the return journey to earth the Prophet Muhammad confirmed that my relationship with Lucia had indeed been an error that must stand corrected.

I felt quite calm and normal throughout this experience, although it was to be several months before I would be given any clue to the nature of the structure I had been taken so far to see.

Soon afterwards I experienced a strong impulse from my ordinary heart to return to Suzanna, but this was immediately countermanded by my inner voice. With this inner response came the clear understanding that from now on such important decisions could only come from the power of God, to which I must surrender in all things. Two weeks later I received that it was now right for me to begin to "repair" my marriage. Within a few days the month of Ramadan began, and Suzanna and I began to spend time together again. In June, shortly after the month of fasting, I sold the apartment in West London and returned home.

Much later I asked Suzanna why she had continued through everything to be there for me. She replied simply, "Because I love you." Although she had felt disappointed and cheated, she went on to say, her own inner feeling always reminded her of the sanctity of her marriage vows.

On returning home I faced a protracted period of convalescence that amounted to a training course in complete surrender. I had to have immense patience. As, no doubt, did Suzanna too!

I still could not read or watch television, and listening to music became all-important to me. A mixture of gentler pop music and the classics sustained me through long hours of outer inactivity. Luckily, Jess and Gyp, our two little dogs, shared my taste in music, as they were my constant companions at this time!

The slightest exertion would shatter my tenuous hold on physical health. I would often overreach my limited strength and feel lost in a kind of no-man's-land of weakness.

In the very worst of these limbo states, at a moment when I felt beyond help, something happened that again suggested that God's own purpose was very much at work in my life. I was rescued from oblivion by an all-powerful latihan, accompanied by a voice saying, "Nothing can interfere with my plan."

Then, one night not long afterward, I was visited by two unidentified figures. They bent over me, and one of them held a mirror to my lips to see if I was still breathing. In the morning I awoke to hear a voice saying, "It has come to our attention that you are very weak right now. But we are here to tell you that you will become very, very strong in the future."

Discussing all this with Sudarto later, his comment may well seem strange to our twentieth-century Western minds. "It is quite usual," he said, "for angels to work in pairs."

A few weeks further into my convalescence, in an early morning latihan, I was taken by the same two companions to choose a new computer. "How nice it would be to have a modern one," I said. "Don't worry," they replied, "It will be the most up-to-date model available, all in one piece."

That night I awoke to observe my two visitors bolting the new computer into my head. "You'll need a week or so to get used to it," they said, and for the next few days I was aware of an unfamiliar, slightly dizzy sensation.

I recognized my new "brain" as soon as I saw it. It was an exact replica in miniature of the edifice I had been taken into space to see, some two months earlier, by the Prophet Muhammad.

BACK IN ACTION

My return to work was a slow process, and at first I could only manage a couple of hours a day. Gradually this increased to half days and eventually to a full working week.

Not that I ever returned to anything like my former total involvement with business. Now I was content to work shorter hours, and I also worked differently. I was no longer *identified* with work. Instead, I remained tuned to what I came to regard as a spiritual pacemaker, an inner regulator, that kept everything in its right place and in perspective.

With my new computer "brain" had come a file drawer crammed full of computer programs in the form of brightly colored film transparencies. The first two related to an important meeting scheduled for a week later. Our most important client at that time had been taken over by a larger group, so that a sizable percentage of our turnover was at risk. It would be my job to convince the new management to retain our services.

This would be my first really tough challenge since my collapse, in terms of dealing with the outside world, and I was by no means confident I was ready for such a confrontation. On entering the boardroom it became at once apparent that the situation was even more daunting than I had anticipated. I could see I was in real danger of being caught in the crossfire between rival management cliques, each fighting for supremacy, if not for their very survival, in the executive shake-up that often accompanies corporate takeovers.

I sat nervously through the preliminaries, feeling vulnerable and unsure of myself after the trauma of the past year. I was all too aware of the dark undercurrents of anxiety, conflict, and ambition in the room, and of the marked hostility on the part of two men in particular toward the potential threat I represented to their roles and to their established ways of doing things. Then it was my turn to be introduced by the chairman as he casually threw me to the lions.

I looked around the room without a thought in my head and with no notes to work from. Suddenly it was as though my new brain switched into action. I felt filled with power and clarity. To my amazement and relief, I gave the performance of my life. I observed myself knitting the meeting together, smoothing ruffled feathers along the way, and delivering a brilliant presentation of our company's irreplaceable expertise and experience in what I perceived to be the exact area of their greatest need.

By the time I finished, all present were in agreement that no other agency would possibly handle their immediate requirements. Winding up the meeting, the chairman thanked me for contributing such a refreshing combination of enthusiasm and professionalism.

Phew!

In fact, this proved to be the first of many similar incidents in the year ahead, in which an increasingly relaxed and dispassionate stance based upon the latihan went hand in hand with success and effectiveness in business. Furthermore, this facility began to manifest itself in the more creative aspects of my work as well, and I was often able to come up with advertising and marketing concepts with very little of the in-depth thought and effort that such projects would usually call for.

Again and again, advertising headlines and marketing strategies would float into my head without any of the customary imaginative brainstorming. These creative solutions would invariably meet with the instant approval of our clients, and this effortless success called to mind the encouraging advice given by Iksan (one of Bapak's earliest helper-ambassadors to the West) not to be afraid of letting go of existing powers in order to be able to regain them from a higher level. I felt I was witnessing the proof of Bapak's assertion that the latihan would eventually permeate our whole being and that the guidance of God would manifest itself in every aspect of our life.

Significantly, the year following my return to the office proved to be our most successful to date. Although I had many other commitments, I was able to bring in more new business than our three sales representatives put together. Despite my more detached approach, things just went my way, but I did not feel I could take personal credit for our success. I knew that it was due entirely to God's blessing and guidance.

THE PUNCH

I   t was at this point during the regeneration process that I received I had experienced the end of a life and death cycle. It was certainly true that I had gone through a death or separation in relation to my former self and ways of being, evidenced by character changes that one of my business partners was later to describe as "huge." In addition to the transformation of my attitude toward work, for example, I could no longer swear, touch alcohol, tell or listen to tasteless jokes, or look at women in an inappropriate way, all of which had hitherto been habitual to me, albeit in varying degrees.

By October 1987 I was making good progress and felt strong and confident enough to take Suzanna on holiday—our first in many years. We chose Crete, where we spent two stress-free weeks relaxing in the sunshine and exploring that lovely island.

Everything seemed to be going well. I was reunited with my wife and getting stronger with every passing week, business was good, and here I was enjoying a delightful break en route to a full recovery.

Surely it was reasonable to assume that, having been put back together again, I could expect to continue going from strength to strength?

Then, while still on holiday I had a dream that seemed at first entirely without content, little more than a source of amusement. Eventually, as I came to recognize the far-reaching significance of its inner meaning, I realized that it was laying down the ground rules that would govern every second of my life for the next couple of years. It could, in fact, easily provide the theme for an entire book, a book without an ending, since it goes to the very heart of staying in touch with the spiritual life while still in this world, this homeland of the lower forces.

In the dream I had just finished cleaning out an enormous cow shed, and it looked spotless. My boss came to inspect my work. "So you're satisfied with this, are you?" he asked me.

I looked around again but could see nothing to complain about, unless you counted a single tiny piece of straw lying at my feet. But even that was perfectly clean and shiny. It looked exactly like a small golden capital letter *I*.

"Come and have a cup of tea," said my boss then, in a very friendly manner.

Over tea, he said, "From now on, whenever it is appropriate for you to say either 'please' or 'thank you' to me, you must say it immediately."

"Sounds easy enough," I thought to myself.

A few minutes later such an occasion arose and I was in the process of formulating the best way to say thank you when, without warning, my boss drew back his fist and punched me in the jaw with all his force, knocking me over backward.

"I said *immediately*," he reminded me.

It wasn't long afterward that the crucial message contained in this dream began to get through to me: that it was vital to stay very close to the fountainhead of a new and deeper spiritual identity; that through awareness I must allow this spiritual source to govern every act and movement, every thought and intention, and every usage of the senses.

I began to find that only through *constant awareness* from moment to moment would this inner contact and control be maintained. If my awareness slipped even for an instant, I would pay a heavy inner price, aptly symbolized by the punch in the dream.

Though it had become clear during my crisis that I had been separated from those lower forces that had previously held sway within me, all it took at that time for those negative influences to reimpose themselves upon my inner feeling was a momentary lapse in awareness. But whereas in the past being governed and manipulated by the lower aspects of my nature had seemed right and normal, now I was able to experience the highly unpleasant and burdensome truth of that state every time I "slipped."

Such a relapse could be triggered merely by using the mildest of swearwords, by joining heedlessly in the enjoyment of a dirty joke, by the temptation to say anything unkind or derogatory about another person, by looking at a woman from the wrong place, or even by making a slightly impatient physical movement—by any act of carelessness in any part of my being, in other words, that caused me to forget and, therefore, lose contact with my inner self.

In the months that followed, the training required by these lessons in awareness were like walking a tightrope or skating on very thin ice. Constant inner attention was called for. As Bapak wrote in his book, *Susila Budhi Dharma* :

> . . . so if a man is inattentive, even for just a moment, then he will instantly become unable to tell one from another of the forces that impose on his inner feeling at such a time.

The process intensified as, later still, the demands of this inner awareness and instant control extended even to my freedom to speak in the first-person pronoun. Its use, now seen to be have been clearly symbolized by the golden capital letter *I* in the dream, was gradually withdrawn from me altogether. Strange and hard though this seemed, I realized by this time that understanding would come only through surrender. I had no choice but to accept and follow what was now clearly more than ever a continually unfolding spiritual path.

During the first phase of this new trial, I found that if I uttered the word *I* (or any other personal pronoun) before 8:45 a.m. or after 5:45 p.m. on weekdays (i.e., outside normal business hours), I would at once become heavily oppressed by negative lower forces, a highly unpleasant condition that could last for several hours and sometimes for a whole day. After a few weeks of this, the restriction was extended to include weekends. Once I had adjusted to that, it was further extended so that I was bound to this extraordinary discipline around the clock.

Except when it arose of itself in latihan, I was unable to use any personal pronoun whatsoever for more than a year, a requirement that called for an unbelievable degree of self-awareness. Try talking normally, or even casually singing the words of just about any popular song, for even a few minutes without saying *I, me, my,* or *mine,* and you'll see what I mean!

Nevertheless, I became adept at conducting conversations without using personal pronouns, speaking of myself either in the third person or in the first person plural when absolutely necessary. Naturally, I felt very self-conscious about this at times, especially when talking to strangers. If I was booking a travel reservation, for example, the clerk would sometimes ask, "So how many people are actually travelling, sir?"

During this time I was somewhat comforted to come across the following remark made by Bapak in Jakarta in August 1973:

> Bapak hopes that you will truly surrender to God almighty and give up your *I*, so that your *I* can really be stripped bare and you can receive what is actually there in your inner self.

And by another one he made in Vancouver in July 1981:

> The word *I* is a very important thing to have and use. But if you misunderstand it or misuse it, or if you are not clear about it, then it can also be very dangerous because we say all the time, "I do this" or "I do that" or "I am able to know this and say that and do that."

But who is "I"?

When we say *I*, it is not at all easy, it is very very difficult to
be clear who is *I* and who is influencing *I* at that moment.

Bapak went on to explain that the purpose of the latihan is to teach
us to experience the separation of our real *I* from all the subordinate
forces that vie for ascendancy within us.

My year and more without personal pronouns was a time of great
suffering, during which no single aspect of my nature was allowed to
masquerade for a moment as my true self. It was a bizarre period, and
I do not know of any other Subud member who has been subjected to
such a constraint. As if by way of compensation, however, I know that
I was also blessed with rare spiritual experiences. In other words,
knowledge of my own nothingness went hand in hand with a con-
sciousness of almighty God's absolute power.

But "I" still had one big lesson to learn before I was given back
my *I*.

Highways and Byways

Throughout 1988 I found that my feelings toward Suzanna were becoming more and more detached. Once again I began to doubt that we would ever have a truly meaningful relationship. Had I acted too hastily in returning to my wife, perhaps out of an unconscious need for emotional support in the wake of my crisis? For over a year I was unable to make any kind of loving approach to her. Sometimes I would awake in the early hours of the morning with a rather fine form of physical arousal, but, having persuaded myself yet again that things were probably over between us, I ignored these impulses.

In January 1989 I travelled alone to Sydney, Australia, for the 8th Subud World Congress. Suzanna had been undecided about accompanying me, and I did not feel moved to urge her to do so. Somehow I knew I had to go, although I also felt very detached and without expectations at the prospect. I was quite surprised, therefore, when the trip turned into a magical two weeks of receiving and sharing with 1,500 Subud brothers and sisters from all over the world. For me, the journey culminated in a four-day stopover in Jakarta on the way back home for a visit to Bapak's grave. This in itself was an experience worth all the travelling involved. Curiously, I had never visited Indonesia during his lifetime.

During the closing weeks of 1988 I had begun to find it increasingly difficult to identify with the interests and aspirations of our advertising and marketing clients, my principal concern. It was as if a switch had been turned off inside me as far as this involvement was concerned. I was sure I was approaching a major change of direction, and several inner "hints" seemed to suggest that this would be connected with going to America. I shared this uncertainty with Andrew and Marcus, my business partners, promising them a firm decision about my future with the company by the time I returned from Congress.

Although I had never been a diarist I was moved before leaving the U.K. to pack a notebook with a view to keeping a journal of my time "down under." Instead, within hours of arriving at the Congress and out of nowhere I felt a strong impulse to write about my experiences of the preceding two years, which I had kept very much to myself in the interim. I spent my first five days and nights in Sydney in something of a creative fever, producing the first draft of the manuscript that was to develop into this book.

In a Ramadan dream of some years before I had stood beside a very animated and enthusiastic Bapak, facing a group comprising what might be termed the "Subud establishment." Bapak called me "Parousia," a name that meant nothing to me and was to remain a mystery for another decade. Then, pointing at me, Bapak said, "This is the man to tell the world about Subud." At the time, as an obscure Subud member immersed in business and the hard-working father of six children, I could not see how such an indication could ever come to reality, although I had no doubt about the truth of its content. Now I connected this with my writing and knew that I had to be free if I were to focus on this book and follow my inner guidance. As soon as I returned to England I withdrew from my business partnerships.

Lucia was also in Sydney for the Congress, having joined Subud during our association and by now well established in the latihan. It had been two years since we parted so abruptly, and it was a great blessing to be presented with this opportunity of healing the wounds and restoring a true sister/brother relationship.

But it was while I was in Australia that I discovered just how vulnerable I still was in my feelings as far as women were concerned. Predisposed by the indications that America would somehow figure prominently in my future, I fell in love yet again, albeit in a very inner way, this time with Rozana, a Subud member from the U.S. who was also in Sydney for the Congress.

Our meeting had been previewed in an overwhelming dream many months before, in which I stood outside a reinforced bunker with solid steel doors at least one foot thick. Within the bunker a nuclear explosion was detonated, and the sheer heat of the blast caused special screws holding the door in place to melt away. The door swung open, and I found myself exposed to the full ferocity of the explosion, which seared through my body, threatening to strip the flesh from my bones. I could barely stand there, teeth clenched, while this mighty wave of concentrated energy passed through me. This dream experience was coupled with an equally powerful latihan the following day which suggested that, once again, love was destined to play an important role in my life.

As soon as I met Rozana [not her real name] I knew that these indications related to her. But, clearly still subservient to a deep emotional lack within myself, I misinterpreted them as positive guidance rather than as warnings, or perhaps simply as a preview of what the future held in store.

The forty-eight hours I spent with Rozana in Sydney were very beautiful and quite free of physical desire or temptation. We experienced a great inner closeness, and I felt sure I had found my soul mate. I returned to England and to the stark contrast of my continuing detachment toward Suzanna. I did not tell her about Rozana; instead, I explained that I felt we were simply unable to make each other happy and that it would be helpful for us to put this to the test by living apart. In view of the fact that we had been so distant from each other for so long, I was surprised at how upset she was by my suggestion. I did what I could to console her and help her to adjust, but two months later I left again, this time to visit Rozana in the United States.

To my dismay, the openness Rozana had shown in Sydney had given way to a defensive mistrust, and the inner sweetness we had experienced together in Sydney did not translate into any semblance of outer reality. Clearly I had made a very big mistake. Later someone reminded me that Bapak had spoken about the need for Subud men and women to take care not to allow the mutual openness of their inner feeling to lead them into errors of this kind. Another brother quoted Bapak's "It is the will of God that man should learn from his mistakes."

This particular mistake had been possible, I am sure, because the drive of an unhealed need within me had become confused with the series of real, if indefinite, indications concerning America. Time was to show that it was certainly right for me to go to the States, even if the circumstances of my first visit were seemingly inappropriate. "All things work together for good," my grandmother was fond of saying, "with those who love the Lord." Although I may have acted prematurely, I had certainly done so in full sincerity.

Nothing Is Impossible for God

I It was becoming obvious that for me "love" was very much a danger zone, although I was still closely identified with the problem and was not quite ready to confront it. Still convinced that my marriage was effectively over—despite being told in latihan by my long-departed father that "marriage is very important"—I left the States immediately after Ramadan and headed for Jakarta with a view to finding a breathing space in which to reorient myself and work on my book. It was in this latter connection that I dropped in for what was to be the first of several conversations with Pak Sudarto Martojudojo.

I was indeed fortunate to be able to spend so much time with Sudarto at this point in my life. He had been a Subud member since the age of 17 and, now 74 years old, was the oldest of Bapak's original helpers. Over the years he had earned the respect and gratitude of countless Subud members for the clarity and insight of his receiving and advice.

When we first met I told him I was writing a book based in part upon my own recent experiences, a book I hoped would reach and speak to "the outside world." He received quietly for a moment and then said, "In an age when technology is advancing and morality is declining, this book will help people to feel open. They will feel, 'Ah, here is a way.'"

To my surprise, he continued, seemingly quite out of context, "In general, the economic condition of Subud members is poor at this time. But God is guiding you so that you can help to arrange and strengthen Subud enterprises."

His words reminded me of a Ramadan dream of some ten years before in which Bapak took me into his private garden and showed me a small group of newly planted conifers. There were perhaps a dozen altogether, neatly laid out in a semicircle. Each young tree represented a Subud enterprise. "You should be selling all of these," he said to me.

Despite Sudarto's unexpected confirmation of this indication, it was to be over a year before it began to be reflected in my outer life.

Very significantly in the light of my second discussion with Sudarto, the night before our next meeting I awoke at around 4 a.m. to feel a beautiful latihan entering through the top of my head. This fine vibration then moved down through my body and manifested in a very pure form of sexual arousal that was quite free of desire or passion, that was in fact very sweet and noble and one hundred per cent spiritual in both origin and direction.

It was during this second talk that, almost in passing, I touched upon the question of my marriage, explaining why I thought it was over. I was completely thrown when Sudarto's response seemed to ignore the neat scenario I had so logically expounded. To begin with, his interpretation of the nuclear explosion dream experience was that it symbolized the worst thing that could happen to me. "But," he added, "even in this extreme situation you were protected by the power of God." This was true: it had certainly proved quite impossible to develop my involvement with Rozana.

Sudarto's next remark reminded me of my 4 a.m. experience of the night before. After receiving about and remarking upon Suzanna's excellent personal qualities, he continued, "In most cases, sexual union arises from the passions. But the best time for union is in fact in the early morning, around 4 a.m., when the passions are at their quietest, but even then *only as a receiving.*" And he went on to point out that at such times it is best to stay as close as possible to the sleeping state so that, hopefully, the nafsu (passions and desires) will not be able to interfere with following the receiving. "When the inner self is strong enough you can do it when you like," he laughed, "but if you are in doubt as to the source of the impulse to make love, it is better not to pursue it."

With these simple words I felt stopped in my tracks. Perhaps I had been drawing entirely the wrong conclusions with regard to the state of my marriage. Were the feelings of emotional detachment and the absence of physical desire merely further aspects of the fundamental changes that were initiated during my crisis?

I began to feel persuaded that this might indeed be the case when Sudarto continued by explaining how a marriage should develop when seen from the spiritual point of view. Although a marriage begins on a heart-to-heart basis, he said, it should then progress to a feeling-to-feeling basis, before deepening to an inner feeling-to-inner feeling basis and thence to a soul-to-soul basis. He also spoke of this progression in terms of developing from the material level, through the vegetable and animal levels, to the human. Only when a marriage has passed through all these stages can it be said to be complete, he remarked, and added, half jokingly, "How can you possibly think of looking for a new wife until the first marriage is complete?"

Bapak often spoke about the quality of received sexual union between husband and wife as potentially the highest form of worship. He explained that when we are no longer controlled by the lower forces, it is possible for the content of our inner feeling to unite with that of our marriage partner and raise it to the level of a complete human being.

Sudarto reaffirmed how much importance Bapak attached to this aspect of the spiritual life and to the need for the inner self and the latihan to participate—indeed predominate—in sexual union. He illustrated this inner reality with a reminiscence of a simple but profound parable from his own time with Bapak.

They were sitting quietly together one day, both men in the latihan state, while Bapak was smoking a cigar. After a while Sudarto became aware that he was beginning to savor the smell of the cigar—whereupon Bapak immediately cautioned him that he, Sudarto, was beginning to allow his enjoyment of the cigar smoke to eclipse his awareness of the latihan.

This simple anecdote is beautifully expressive of the importance of staying close to the latihan in everything, although I must admit that it took me a while fully to appreciate its relevance to the subject under discussion!

As a direct result of Sudarto's advice, I suggested that Suzanna join me in Jakarta, where we talked more openly than we had for years about our marriage and agreed to get back together yet again. During our stay in Jakarta I took Suzanna to meet Sudarto, who was clearly delighted to meet her. "Something beautiful," he said, "sometimes needs time to come to fruition."

I must acknowledge, however, that the reunion was based more upon my trust in the wisdom of Sudarto's advice, and upon his reminder that "nothing is impossible for God," than upon any deep inner conviction on my part. Thanks to Sudarto, I had begun to discern that marriage is an integral part of the spiritual life, that it can be seen as a sacrosanct arena for living out our spiritual evolution. "Divorce," I read somewhere recently, "rocks the throne of God."

But there was no immediate and miraculous change in the inner quality of our life together, and the final nature and destiny of our relationship remained somehow unresolved. It was to be many more months before I would begin to realize how deeply connected I am to Suzanna. And how much I love and value her.

By this time I was back in California, burning to tell the world about the latihan and pursuing my belief that this is where my story should be published.

I began to work with Susannah Clarke, a Subud member—and editor—living in San Diego. Susannah played a unique dual role in my life at that time: that of patient editor and caring friend. A sensitive "midwife" both to that stage of the transition I was then experiencing and to the manuscript that reflected it, it was she who helped me to see that at that stage my story had no ending: I still could not say "I" and I had still not completely resolved my feelings toward my wife.

It was in a sudden burst of illumination after one of our work sessions that I came to see that I had been subject to a life-long feeling of deep loneliness, a longing for perfection, which for years had driven me blindly in search of love and fulfillment in people and situations outside myself. I also saw that, although I had always unconsciously projected the capacity to meet this need onto my work and onto others, it was actually a lack that could only be resolved within my own being by God himself; that only he could be perfect. And I remembered how, in the depths of my crisis, agonizing over what I saw as my need for the "perfect woman," my inner voice had told me, "She must first arise within you."

Suzanna had never stood a chance.

The next day, reflecting upon this realization, what I can only regard as a miraculous change, or at least a very mysterious one, took place in my attitude toward Suzanna. From deep within me, from my true self, I began to declare aloud that *I* loved her. Suddenly, I was able to freely use the personal pronoun that had been denied me for so long.

Over the next few days I discovered that the use of the personal pronoun had been completely restored to me, a marvel somehow borne of love.

One night soon after my return to England, as we lay together in the darkness, I suddenly perceived that the woman I held in my arms was still the sweet and lovely person I had first loved over three decades ago; that, despite all the years of selfless support she had given me, she was still the same youthful, fresh, and precious person.

I drew this young girl closer, and we made love.

Afterwards, as we lay quietly, I became aware that we were travelling together in our inner selves to a far distant place, where we joined a small group of people standing at an open door, watched over by an angel. As I looked at the angel's face I was filled with joy, and the words "love, love, love" arose within me, an anthem of praise and thanksgiving.

Back in my body, still singing my song of love, I turned over and fell asleep. I had found my perfect woman. And it was so good to be home.

Part II. I Live, Yet Not I....

Forward in the Light

Perhaps it was impossible for my mind to *understand* the spiritual reality of what was happening to me during my crisis because the spiritual realm is beyond man's ordinary understanding. But by the time my story had finally "ended" it was impossible *not* to see that the process had brought about a complete change of inner being—or at least a change of the ruling power within.

Although it had been a time of great weakness and incapacitation, at my lowest I had received, "You will be restored to *his* strength." This had echoed, I felt, both that lovely verse from 2 Corinthians, "My strength is made perfect in weakness," and Christ's own "Whomsoever would have his life must lose it."

When I had begun to emerge from the crisis state, I had been fascinated to observe that it was necessary for me to receive from within how to move all over again in latihan, almost as if I were beginning my spiritual training from scratch. It took me several weeks, for example, simply to be able to stand upright again and take short, tentative steps. It was months before I could move really freely from within: before I could walk, run, dance, laugh and sing.

With the crisis behind me and my book taking shape, constant prayer to his name would arise effortlessly of itself within my being—not as a product of my will, heart, or mind, but as a natural extension and expression of the latihan itself.

Every day my inner self would pray spontaneously, "I am so happy and joyful in your presence. You are so wise and wonderful. Thank you for all your grace and majesty unto me." Or, in a glorious affirmation of oneness, "You are everything to me, and I belong to you completely."

If I needed encouraging, I would be reminded, "Be happy and joyful in the Lord. Everything is coming through to you from him. There is nothing to worry about." And I was continually enjoined from within to "go forward in the light." This, I knew, meant to *live* the latihan.

Increasingly, a spirit of detachment flavored my life, both inwardly and outwardly, coupled (paradoxical though it may sound) with a deep love and compassion. Toward Suzanna I felt inwardly united, protective and committed; toward my children I felt a deep but objective caring; toward Jess, my dog and unquestioning companion,

I felt responsible but uninvolved; toward my brothers and sisters in Subud I felt a strong but impersonal bond.

Looking back over 1989 and 1990 it is clear that, for me, these had been years of questing and discovery, financed by the sale of my business interests. Certainly it had been a time for journeys, both inner and outer, including visits to Australia, America, Indonesia, Mexico, and Portugal. Mostly I travelled alone.

In September 1989 I made my second trip to the U.S. with a view to going forward with the book. At that stage my manuscript was simply a story of spiritual crisis and recovery—albeit one that I sincerely believed merited publication as a personal account of the latihan in action—and I was daunted to discover that it would not be easy to interest a mainstream publisher in a manuscript of this nature. But, as my receivings continued to deepen and multiply, they also began to indicate that my *book* was in any case far from complete: that it had a wider purpose, and that its "ending" had only been the beginning of a bigger story I had yet to fully experience before I could fully tell.

But of course this amazing grace we call the latihan does not stand still.

Medugorje

O ne night toward the end of my second visit to America I received that something to do with Christ would shortly come about that would cause me to rewrite the *beginning* of my book. On yet another occasion I was awakened by the word *Messiah*, coupled with an indication that I would shortly encounter something that would somehow "intersect" with my own experience to form a cross, and that this intersection would also show me how to write the *ending*.

Two weeks later I was moved to go to a local Catholic bookstore where I was electrified to hear for the first time about the current apparitions of Our Lady which have been occurring at Medugorje, Yugoslavia, since June 24, 1981.

At the heart of the Medugorje phenomenon are thousands of appearances over many years that, it is said, Mary has made to a small group of young villagers. These events have been accompanied and reinforced by hundreds of more general visitations and other supernatural events, similar to those associated with Our Lady's appearances at Fatima in 1917, which have been witnessed by many others, locals and visitors alike.

I was stunned by the parallels between Our Lady's messages at Medugorje and the words of Bapak, and by the relationship between Mary's call for a return to God and the dispensation of grace that is the latihan. I knew that this was the intersection I had been alerted to expect.

Comparing the messages attributed to Mary at Medugorje with the transcripts of Bapak's many talks around the world, I was repeatedly struck by their similar content, often expressed in the very same words.

Both had reminded us that there is only one God, and both had called for complete surrender to him. In an interview recorded in January 1983, Mirjana, one of the young people to whom Mary has appeared, said, "She has always pointed out that there is only one God and that people have separated themselves. You cannot believe; you are not a Christian, if you do not respect other religions."

Like Bapak—and in company with all the masters from all the traditions across all the centuries—Our Lady had spoken of opening the *inner self* to the Lord, so suggestive of the Subud latihan of inner surrender and awareness. And in Our Lady's tireless reminders of the value of constant prayer "from the heart" and regular fasting there was an unmistakable echo of Bapak's ceaseless encouragement to "stay close to the latihan" and to consider the need for *prihatin* (self-denial) and the annual fast of Lent or Ramadan.

Just as Bapak had urged Subud members to "put your latihan into practice" and follow the guidance they receive so that God's grace will not be wasted, so Mary had implored her seers to "live my messages" so that her mission and God's purpose may be crowned with success. At Medugorje the Blessed Virgin had said that her message is for "all mankind," precisely the phrasing so often used by Bapak in relation to Subud.

❀ ❀ ❀

Although Bapak always discouraged proselytizing, he often said that the time would come when there would be a dramatic increase in the number of people following the latihan.

I find it extraordinary in this age of instant global communications that the existence and availability of the miracle of the latihan is completely unknown to the vast majority of the world's population. This state of affairs contrasts markedly with Bapak's words in Washington, D.C., in July 1981, when he said, "It is a very great mistake if this spiritual exercise does not spread to the whole of mankind; if this spiritual exercise gets stuck with just a few people here and there."

Certainly, the latihan would seem to have been "stuck with just a few people here and there" for some time, and from the outset my purpose in writing this book had stemmed from an instinctive feeling that it was now right that Subud should be brought to the attention of the world at large as a matter of urgency.

One aspect more than any other of my Subud/Medugorje "intersection" served to reinforce my original sense of pressing commitment to produce the book: the correlation I saw between Mary's stark warnings of pending global devastation and Bapak's occasional, more ambivalent allusions to this possibility. Combined with my own persistent and hitherto unshared receiving in this regard, it was this immediate recognition that also helped to broaden my perception of my book's message, and imbued me with an even greater sense of responsibility and urgency toward expressing it.

Mary is constantly reminding us "how strong Satan has become and how he has been able to lead millions into darkness at this time." Bapak, too, spoke of the enormous power now wielded by the forces of materialism, which he also identified as the satanic level. He frequently suggested that it is precisely because its grip upon man has created such a dangerous situation in this day and age that almighty God has, as it were, mounted a rescue effort by making his own cleansing power available to us directly through the latihan.

It is a matter of history that the appearances of Our Lady have often coincided with eras of spiritual darkness. Her mission at such times has invariably been to warn, to comfort, and to renew faith. But in the past such manifestations have been relatively short-lived, sometimes limited to a single vision or perhaps to a few days or weeks; never have they persisted for anything like the duration of her appearances at Medugorje, and never with such sustained regularity and intensity.

When I first heard about Medugorje, it was reported that Mary had been appearing there virtually every day for no less than nine years— surely, I felt, a measure of the extreme peril facing our world today.

I read that Mary had imparted certain secrets to her seers, many of which relate to catastrophes that are destined to strike "soon," and some of which can be averted or alleviated through prayer, fasting, and penance. Other tragedies are altogether certain and cannot be mitigated at all, representing possibly the only redemption for a Godless world. She has indicated that the supreme disaster, defined in an officially recognized revelation at Akita, Japan, in 1973, as "a punishment greater than the deluge," will be preceded by three warnings to the world. These, said Mary at Medugorje, will be followed by a visible sign, after which "those who are still alive will have little time for conversion." She then said, "Life in the world will change and afterwards men will believe like in ancient times."

Bapak, too, had frequently contrasted today's widespread lack of real belief in God with the deep faith of men of old, but it is hard to imagine a general return to the simplicity and values of the ancients without a correspondingly dramatic catharsis in human affairs.

Not everyone agrees that the chastening to be visited upon erring mankind will necessarily take the form of a third world war or an immense natural catastrophe. There are those who believe that the words of warning used both in biblical and in twentieth century revelation are allegorical: that perhaps they symbolize purely economic disasters; that perhaps they represent a battle of ideologies; that perhaps they refer to conflict and changes that will take place within the very hearts of men and women.

But one of my own warning receivings had begun with the statement that "Nation shall rise against nation...," and, even as I was writing, the conflict in the Persian Gulf was demonstrating once again just how quickly and easily our world can be brought to the edge of the abyss, and reminding us that for thousands of years the Middle East has been posited as the venue for Armageddon, the final struggle between the forces of good and evil.

Although Bapak stopped short of saying that the world is definitely heading for a global conflagration, he too often reminded us that our planet has never before been in such great danger. The nearest he came to this, as far as I am aware, was in Jakarta in June 1984 when he said, "If Bapak told you what he knows, you would all feel depressed, so it is better not to talk about it." I also recall him saying that if just three percent of the world's population came to Subud, then peace and harmony would prevail. And, on another occasion, that in the event of a cataclysm, Subud would be preserved on earth.

Much of my own receiving certainly carries with it the definite implication that the world is heading for upheaval. During the Ramadan of 1990 I received two clear indications concerning the end of this world as we know it. In the first, I was shown that there would be three days of global turmoil, the first of which would be hardest to bear because of the "very strong winds that would blow." In the second, a dream, the winds had started to blow and I was trying to make others aware of the fact. I couldn't get through to them, however, and it was shown to me that those who would not accept the reality and meaning of the winds were among those not destined to survive. Although this dream was frightening, it was not a nightmare; I woke from it feeling calm, detached, and strong.

It must be acknowledged that such indications could be interpreted either literally or symbolically, the latter representing perhaps the spiritual death that awaits those who are not willing to surrender to almighty God. I had one particularly strong receiving that could just about fit both interpretations, in which I awoke one night to hear a loud voice, full of portent, say, "God is not yet ready to *stamp* his authority on man."

In encountering the intersection between my own experience and the phenomenon of Medugorje, I sensed that somehow both my life and my book were moving beyond the merely personal. Moved from within by the latihan to pledge total obedience to God, I knew that I could only follow.

As soon as I could arrange it, I was en route for Yugoslavia.

PILGRIMAGE

I t is difficult to imagine how Medugorje must have appeared to the visitor before 1981—except by comparison with neighboring hamlets—because the original character of the village has been totally eclipsed by the constant attention it receives from the outside world.

Scores of buses and taxis jam its streets, parked alongside dozens of look-alike souvenir shops, all competing for the foreign exchange of each day's quota of the thousands of visitors whose English, Irish, American, German, French, and Italian voices somehow meld in the lingua franca of their common purpose.

Yet none of this detracts from the immediate impression that something truly special is happening there. The church itself, set well back from the road, stands aloof from the commercialism as if to endorse this perception.

The church, simple but impressive in design and superbly floodlit after dark, was crowded throughout my five-day stay, as service succeeded service in all the languages necessary to minister to the multinational influx. A public address system relayed the proceedings to those outside. The large square surrounding the church was usually as crowded as the church itself: with impromptu groups praying together or listening to their own priest or guide; with dozens of people saying, or waiting for, confession in the open air; with individuals seeking solitude either on the benches provided or in the adjacent grassy areas.

As soon as I had found somewhere to stay, I dumped my suitcase and hurried to the church. I immediately met Inge, a Danish pilgrim in her mid-sixties whom I had seen in a dream the night before. A recent convert to Catholicism, she was on her second visit to Medugorje. Somehow our eyes met in immediate recognition, and we began to talk. She tried without success to describe the grace she had experienced on her previous visit, her tears of joy far more eloquent than her words.

Inge was able to give me a good impression of the local scene and, in particular, spoke with keen anticipation of Our Lady's monthly message. It seemed that, although Mary appears every day to the young seers and gives them a personal message, on the 25th of each month her message is a special one for the whole world and is posted in the church vestibule. By a happy coincidence I had arrived in Medugorje on the afternoon of Tuesday, October 24.

That evening I received a strong latihan, very loving and worshipful, and that night I had two clear dreams: one in which Bapak came very close to me, and another in which I was shown the cover for this book.

❀ ❀ ❀

The following morning I walked up Krizevac Hill to the giant concrete cross that dominates the area, a place of miracles and apparitions. It was a grueling climb up an extremely steep, rocky path, and is an important act of penance and sacrifice for many pilgrims. Some pray aloud as they climb, despite their shortness of breath, and not a few make the ascent barefoot. The view from the top is breathtaking: one direction overlooks a stunning panorama of Medugorje and its environs, a carpet of intricate design spread far below; another reveals a mountain range that stretches into an ethereal infinity in folds of purple and blue—mystical, mysterious, and achingly beautiful.

Scattered across the summit are innumerable wooden crosses, brought from every point of the compass. I made my way to a quiet hollow, where I stood alone in a latihan of praise before falling to my knees in thanksgiving. Appropriately enough, in view of my own recent travels in America, the cross erected in that place had been carried overland across the U.S.

Back in the village for lunch, I relaxed in the warm sunshine, reflecting on what I saw around me and looking forward to the posting of Our Lady's message later in the day.

By now I had begun to find the nonstop broadcasting of services, particularly sermons, a little irksome. The practice, it seemed to me, left little space for inner quietness, for the cultivation of "that peace which the world cannot give." Presumably most people are only here for a day or so and often only for a few hours, I noted in my journal, and then return to the rat race of modern life. Is the power of God really touching and changing many of these people under these circumstances, I asked myself. Everyone is sincerely reaching out here, but how many are making a real inner contact? Outwardly they are praying, praying, praying, but where are they coming from, and are they really going within?

I heard one priest urging his flock to spend the whole day on one prayer, concentrating on each individual word, one at a time. Asking in my journal for protection from and forgiveness for any misunderstanding on my part or tendency toward spiritual pride, I wondered how this could possibly lead to the *inner* prayer Our Lady is calling for.

I couldn't wait to get to the church that Wednesday evening to read Our Lady's message. I felt full of the latihan as I made my way across the square, the inner prayer pulsing stronger than ever, "Father, Father, Father."

That message is reproduced below. The italics are mine.

> Dear children. Today also I am inviting you
> to prayer. I am always inviting you *but you are*
> *still far away.* Therefore, from today, decide
> seriously to dedicate time to God. I am with you
> and I wish to teach you to pray with the heart.
> In prayer with the heart you shall encounter God.
> Therefore, little children, pray, pray, pray.
> Thank you for having responded to my call.

If I had already caught occasional glimpses of what I saw as the connection between Medugorje and the latihan, it was this message—and particularly those telling words, *but you are still far away*—that brought the correlation into sharp focus.

At Medugorje, Mary is calling for a profound human renewal, a deep and lasting change in the very hearts of people everywhere. She has been pleading for this transformation for over nine years, warning of a nemesis that will be upon us "soon."

With the latihan, God is making possible the spiritual revolution that Mary is urging, opening an inner door to the response and surrender that all mankind is being called upon to make at this critical time.

Medugorje is calling people to God. Calling, calling, calling. *But we are still far away.*

The latihan is a living contact with his power. *Bringing him close.*

The Second Coming

The next day, Thursday, my third in Medugorje, I seemed to drift through time and place, flowing from moment to moment without plan or intention. After lunch, to my surprise, I experienced a latihan of tears and heaviness, and then slept. I awoke feeling full of sorrow and close to weeping. The feelings of aloneness and alienation from the throng around me had never been stronger.

I soon realized that my sadness had been due to a renewed awareness of my smallness compared to the greatness of almighty God—something of a throwback to my crisis state. By evening my spiritual self was able to worship God in a very beautiful latihan: "He is everything. All praise and worship be to him. From him alone can come whatever may be needed. God be praised and worshipped above all."

From past experience I knew that this *total* surrender, this reminder of my *complete* dependence upon God, could well be a prelude to an important receiving.

In the morning I was awakened by a vision of Christ. I received instantly and completely how the beginning of *Revelation Subud* should be reoriented:

**It should be *Christ*-centered and should bear
witness to the truth that the latihan is a manifestation
of the Second Coming.**

So This Is Love

I still had a day and a half to spend in Medugorje, and by now I was looking forward to returning to the five-star luxury of my Dubrovnik hotel with its full English breakfasts! I drifted through Friday, impatient to be on my way. I spent the first part of Saturday morning in much the same aimless way until around 11 o'clock, when I started back to my room to pack for a 3 p.m. departure.

Along the way, I chanced upon a group of pilgrims gathered to listen to Mirjana, one of the visionaries, an attractive young lady in her early twenties who works for a local travel agency. I had a shorthand pad with me and was able to take verbatim notes of what was said. She began by apologizing for the fact that she had very little free time from her job that day. Speaking through an interpreter, she then made a short opening statement before inviting questions from her audience.

Mirjana: Our Lady regards everyone the same, those who
            go to church and those who do not. She regards
            herself as the mother of all, those who are close to
            God and those who are not.

Question: Did Our Lady mention anything about the Eastern
            religions?

Mirjana: She said that we are all her children, all people.
            We ourselves made religions; we divided ourselves.
            Jesus is the Savior of all, and it is the role of
            Christianity to lift up the other religions.

Question: What does Our Lady mean by conversion? From
            atheism to Christianity? From other branches of
            Christianity to Catholicism? Or what?

Mirjana: Conversion actually means to turn your back on
            sin and walk toward God. It does not mean leaving
            one denomination and transferring to another. Start
            praying with the heart, walking closer and closer to
            God the Father.

The remaining questions concerned such areas of general interest as Our Lady's actual appearance, and the short exchange was soon over. It was around noon when I sat down to make the following note in my journal: "I was getting quite uncomfortable here among all these intense people, what with the constant formal services and prayer by rote. How beautiful to round off my visit by seeing and hearing Mirjana. She is so open, simple and relaxed—so Subud-like, somehow. Afterwards there was some intangible, other-worldly quality and beauty in the air, and even now I feel moved to tears of love and sweetness."

I am not entirely sure what happened next. I remember getting to my feet to resume my walk back to my room when I was suddenly and completely overwhelmed by a pure love that defies description. I ran blindly into the field next to the church where I sobbed without restraint in a condition of utter abandonment before almighty God. I was totally possessed by a love that caused something in my chest to melt. It was like being opened for the second time, but in a new way. *This* love was *everything*.

I prostrated myself in joy and worship as the latihan coursed through me—"Maria, Christus, Allah hu-akbar [God is almighty]"—its boundless grace merging with the mystery of Medurgorje.

There was no longer any separation between the two. I was at one with all creation, and I *knew* that God is love. The *intersection* was complete. My tears glistened on the grass of Medugorje, and this perfect love flowed out to all around me.

I stood as the latihan poured through me: "Praise the Lord, O my soul. All that is within me, bless his holy name."

Whereupon, from my ordinary heart, transformed: *How can I bear to leave this special place and all these dear people?* And the inner reply, "The Lord is with you."

Then, through the sweet tears of this almost unbearable love, I was moved anew from within to pledge total service to God and to promise to follow wherever he might lead.

PAROUSIA

I n May 1990 I travelled to the United States for the third time, once again following my guidance that this is where my book should first be published. As I had been guided to expect, Medugorje had indeed shown me—at least in a sense—how my story should begin and, by its very "intersection," end. I had completed my pilgrimage; now I had my heart set on completing my *manuscript*.

During the early hours of my first night in America, I awoke to find myself confronting an apparition of Our Lady. I sat up and she advanced to my bedside. Like the sweetest of mothers, she gently placed her fingers over my mouth and said, "Your book won't come out yet." Then she paused before going on to confirm the rightness of my being in America: "You have begun to sing with new Subud friends. And I approve of this."

I was intensely disappointed that yet again it seemed I must put my book aside. I felt completely thrown by Our Lady's intervention, and it took me at least a week to recover an attitude of acceptance and patience. Eventually I came to feel that the significance of Mary's remark concerned its timing, and, following my guidance and testing, I remained in the U.S. and began to work with a few small, struggling Subud enterprises.

This was in harmony with the second part of Mary's message, as well as with Sudarto's comment about enterprises that had seemed so out of context when I had met with him in Jakarta.

Following one's spiritual guidance is not always easy;   it is sometimes open to misinterpretation on the ordinary level and does not always bestow instant understanding of its full meaning or purpose. It calls for faith and courage—especially when one feels one has none!— and even a willingness to make mistakes, trusting in God to correct the course where necessary. For the past few years I had been called upon to try and live such a life, often unsure of my direction and destination, but always seeking to "go forward in the light."   It wasn't until several months after my experiences in Medugorje that I began to feel that everything was falling into place; that, by the grace and will of an all-merciful God, I could see his way for me a little more clearly.

When I had been deeply in crisis, well over a year before I had the first impulse to write this book, the figure of Christ had suddenly appeared in front of me during latihan. "I will write the foreword to your book," he said to me. He then paused and fixed me with a long, piercing look. "And that means," he continued, "that it will be big." At the time this meant absolutely nothing to me, and I virtually forgot about it in the ensuing year. With *Revelation Subud* nearing completion, however, I would remember this experience from time to time and wonder about my book's "missing foreword."

Only now, a month after I had seen the apparition of Mary, did I come across the little-known quotation with which this book begins. Bapak's affirmation that the spiritual exercise of Subud is "the reality of Christ coming down to human beings themselves at this time" dovetailed precisely with my receiving at Medugorje. I was thrilled to discover this passage, which I had turned to immediately in the middle of an entire book dedicated to a selection of Bapak's sayings. Soon afterwards I had a clear dream in which I saw that extract at the front of my book, and I knew that the Bapak quotation was what the "foreword" promised by Christ had symbolized.

Although for years I had uttered the name *Christus* in latihan, not since I was a child had I experienced any real sense of the validity of the person of Christ or indeed of the religion that is named after him. In late 1989, however, I became aware of the emergence within me of a great mystery.

It began when I awoke to find myself saying aloud, "The *coming* of the Christ," and continued throughout 1990 with an increasing awareness of the *reality* of the Christ.

My spiritual exercise became ever deeper, and at the end of one particularly profound latihan, I received, "The Christ is in you to his full power," to which I responded: "I know that *I* have to go—for *Him*." I pledged yet again to follow wherever he might lead, and received, "Just surrender everything to me."

I felt heavy and disoriented for the next few days, blocked by seemingly impassable fear and suffering. My nights were full of latihan which slowly began to clear my deathlike state, and once I awoke to feel both my hands held in a firm but unseen grip.

When the darkness finally lifted I received a latihan of great sweetness and consolation and knew that I was beloved of God.

During my crisis I had had a dream in which I had been cruising from deep in space toward earth, but it was not the ordinary me. I was aglow with glory, with extraordinary light and power blazing from and through me. I was moving at a very steady pace, as if in accordance with some pre-ordained plan or timescale. I wore what seemed to be a stiff cape that protruded outward on each side like partly folded wings. (When I had mentioned this experience to Sudarto in Jakarta, he had replied rather sharply, "First you have to pass through all the other levels," as if to caution me against the risk of getting inflated ideas about my spiritual progress!)

In September 1990 I had a dream in which my skin was beginning to burst at the seams, revealing nothing but light and power within. In a spontaneous latihan not long afterwards, I experienced what I can only describe as *a complete identification with the Christ within me.*

This *single* episode, which lasted for about half an hour, felt like the consummation and purpose of all my experiences until that point. It imbued me with fresh inspiration and a new perspective with which to return to the manuscript I had set aside after the apparition in May. Even though I had been working on this book for nearly two years, I felt that only now could I see clearly what it was all about and where it had long been leading from the very beginning. In all my prior experiences, both before, during and immediately after I went to Medugorje, I had seen and heard the person of Christ in the form of visions separate from and external to my own being. Now I was beginning to experience a literal oneness with him as an *inner* reality.

I awoke early one morning in December 1990 to see my body composed entirely of blazing light.

At this stage I had more or less ended my book with the conclusion of my pilgrimage to Medugorje. Although my inner experiences continued to develop in delicate and intimate harmony with the being of Christ, I felt that I neither cared nor dared to express them. But when I showed my developing manuscript to a few Subud friends, I was encouraged to find that it seemed to give them confidence to share with me their own similar, if not identical, experiences. One in particular, a film maker, told me she had experienced the reality of oneness with Christ within herself more than fifteen years before, shortly after she had been opened. She had rarely found it possible to speak of this experience to anyone else.

Like her, I had found it impossible to *speak* of these deeply personal, precious, and ostensibly incredible things to more than one or two people. That I am now sharing as much as possible with whoever may be moved to read my story is because I came to realize that it was not enough for me to have *received* that the latihan is a manifestation of the Second Coming, or indeed to have experienced the reality of it. I knew that the only way I could *bear witness* to it was by having the courage to include those experiences in this account.

I realize that no words of mine can penetrate this ineffable mystery. In seeking to express the inexpressible, I can do no better than fall back upon the simple eloquence of St. Paul. His *"I live, yet not I, but Christ liveth in me"* is, in my experience, given new life two thousand years later in this wondrous latihan: in this spiritual exercise in which I move and laugh and sing and love and worship. In which I move—yes. And yet not I . . .

My experiences have continued to affirm the validity of Paul's vision. In one, a voice in the night said to me, "Christ is the strength in you." In another, a twofold experience, I was first made aware of the Christ in me reaching out, often in quite small ways, to touch and help others, and, then, of the Christ in others reaching out to touch and help me.

In retrospect, I recognize that it was the flowering within me of this deepest and purest of identities that finally broke the pattern that had kept my lonely, fearful "ordinary heart" so desperately ready to look for love and comfort from women. My childlike fears and needs were eclipsed by the emergence of my true self: it is only because I am ever stronger and more complete in him that I am able ever more truly to love and share and serve as husband, father, friend, and brother.

Jesus said, "I am the way, the truth, and the life." He urged the world to take up its cross and follow him, saying, "I and the Father are one," and "No man cometh unto the Father but by me."

I am sometimes given to experience these truths for myself in my latihan—this spiritual exercise in which *I* am *him,* and in which I know that I am an extension of God's will and purpose—although I would not have the temerity to seek to express these mysteries were it not for the direct simplicity of Bapak himself. It is not that almighty God *himself* is within us, he explained in Vancouver in July 1981, but rather that the *power* of God is within everything he created within the whole universe. He continued:

The only difference is which of his creatures are aware of the presence of the power of God and which of them are not aware of it. This is the distinction that becomes apparent in the latihan. As a result of the latihan . . . you are able to become aware of the presence, the manifestation, of God's power within you…Within our being this power enables us to get to know and to feel our own true nature and personality …like a life within your life, and deeper than your everyday life. It is *this* which you must worship. It is *this* which you must magnify. It is *this* which must be your God. Because there is nothing else from which you can learn. *There is nothing else that you can follow except this reality that is within you.*

In March 1990, I spent ten days in Jakarta to attend the final ceremony commemorating Bapak's death, held exactly one thousand days after his passing. While I was there I received deeply within myself that my name should be changed to *Emmanuel*, almost exactly three years after the experience in which I had heard Bapak say that one day he would tell me my *real* name.

One month later, and several months after my visit to Medugorje, I learned the meaning of the *other* name Bapak had called me—in the dream of ten years before in which he had said I would be "the man to tell the world about Subud."

Quite by chance, I discovered that the Greek word *Parousia* meant "Second Coming." It was only then that I realized how Bapak must have foreseen that, in writing this book, I would be guided to link the latihan with the Second Coming of Christ, a reality in which *all* men and women may choose to participate here and now.

STOP PRESS

To confirm the universality of Subud, or the fact that Subud is
truly something that God wills for mankind at this time,
Bapak remembers a story that he heard a long time ago when
he was in France. It seems that in France there is a place of
pilgrimage for Christians where it is said that the Virgin
Mary once appeared and that many people who go there are
cured of their illnesses. At one point there were two women to
whom the Virgin Mary appeared in that place and, among
many other things, the Virgin told the women that one day a
man would come from the Orient to France, a man who
would have the Muslim religion but nevertheless wear modern
clothes and would not wear a beard or mustache. And he will
be the one who will be able to show Christians the right way.
—Bapak. Jakarta. July 25,1976

I n August 1990 the Persian Gulf crisis began to unfold.
In November 1990 Father Stefano Gobbi, founder of the Marian
Movement of Priests, who has been receiving regular guidance directly
from Our Lady since 1972, received the following message from Mary,
especially for America:

Now I announce to you that the hour has come for
the chastisement predicted by me at Fatima and
contained in that part of the secret which has not yet
been revealed. You must be apostles and proclaim
with strength and courage the gospel of Jesus.
Illuminate the world in these times of great darkness
with the light of your faith, your holiness, and your love.

In January 1991, just as this book was about to go to press, the confrontation in the Persian Gulf developed into war.

On January 25, 1991, in her monthly message to the world at Medugorje, Our Lady said:

> Today, like never before, I invite you to prayer.
> Your prayer should be a prayer for peace. Satan
> is strong and wishes not only to destroy human life
> but also nature in the planet on which you live.

Mary's warnings at Fatima in 1917 of a second world war and of the error that would spread from an atheistic Russia were duly realized in full. And there has always been considerable speculation that the suppressed "third secret of Fatima," intended by Our Lady to be released in 1960, spoke of even worse to come.

Since first hearing about Medugorje, I have discovered that there is an abundance of Marian-based corroboration on all sides that the day of reckoning is not far off. The import is always the same: time is fast running out, and if mankind does not turn back to God we face a disaster more terrible than we can possibly imagine: the "end of the world" that has always been inextricably linked both in scripture and in revelation old and new with the Second Coming of Christ.

In 1958 John Bennett, a Roman Catholic and one of the original British Subud members responsible for introducing Subud to the West, received that it was "the will of God that Islam and my Church should become one." When he asked who could possibly bring about such a unification, he received, "Mary."

Bapak, too, frequently pointed to the essential unity of Christianity and Islam. From a spiritual standpoint, he said, the two religions *intersected like a cross* to make one whole—exactly the wording I had received with regard to my own "intersection" with Medugorje. And although not many non-Muslims are aware of the fact, the persons of Jesus and Mary are both revered in Islam. The Prophet Muhammad himself spoke of the "Antichrist" who would cause great corruption on earth in the latter days, but who will die at the hands of Jesus, returning to lead the believers in prayer.

It had been Mary's wish that the third secret of Fatima be released to the world in 1960—no less than 43 years after she delivered it. Many have wondered about the significance and purpose of this time lapse; in fact, this proved to be the very time when the West was in the earliest stages of its awareness of the presence on earth of the latihan.

I have been careful in these pages to refrain from personal speculation and theorizing, but in this particular I feel it incumbent upon me to point to this seeming "coincidence." The early sixties were heady days for we hundreds of new Subud members scattered around the globe. We knew that something momentous was taking place, and half expected that millions more would soon recognize and respond to the reality of the latihan. We would not have been surprised if the whole world had been changed within five years!

The Catholic world, too, was in a state of high expectation, keenly awaiting the disclosure of the secret of Fatima. But it was suppressed, and to this day has not been released.

I cannot help but reflect upon the relative timing of these two spiritual events, both so full of significance and potential for humanity. We can but guess at the immense opportunity for spiritual renewal, for the birth of a true brotherhood of man, represented by their reciprocity: on the one hand, Mary's message at Fatima, channeled through the Christian Church, and, on the other, the presence of the latihan, made available originally through a Muslim. We can only speculate upon the extent and the consequences of this apparent circumvention of God's will, and the terrible deprivation that would seem to have been inflicted upon mankind at a time of his greatest need.

The tragedy in the Middle East is compounded daily, and on all sides the politicians deliver earnest arguments to support their motives and actions. Many of them may well be as sincere and well-meaning as they can possibly be. Nevertheless, I am left with the impression that the inexorable flow of events is way beyond their control; that their "decisions" are futile gestures in the face of the onward march of a Destiny to which they are blind.

The war in the Persian Gulf may prove to be quite short-lived. But, no matter how soon it may end, it will no doubt have caused the death of many thousands of human beings, and is bound to have incalculable long-term repercussions. Whether or not it proves to be the beginning of the "final chastening" predicted by Mary, it most certainly fits with her warnings of a succession of disasters on the road to a fearful climax.

During my spiritual crisis I had a vision in which I found myself confronting an agitated group of major world leaders, about twenty-five in all. They were all talking at once, justifying their policies and explaining how much they had achieved. When they were finally quiet, I simply asked them, "But is the world a better place?"

The message for our time, surely, is that only the power of God himself can guide us out of the darkness of materialism and conflict into the light of the true human realm, where—if it is not too late—we may yet surrender to him in helping to make this world a better place: a new kind of place, where we will walk with him in love and unity, brotherhood and peace.

This partnership with him is available to us *now*—in the spiritual exercise of Subud. And, given what I feel blessed to have received, I cannot conceive of a path that could be more pure and powerful than this manifestation of the Second Coming of Christ, this direct contact with "the vibration that is the basis of the whole universe."

February 1991

Subud Contact Addresses

You may well find an entry for your nearest group in the local telephone directory under *Subud*. In case not, the national offices for most of the English-speaking countries are given below.

Subud Australia
GPO Box 1440
Sydney
NSW 2001

Subud New Zealand
4/6 Curran Street
Herne Bay
Auckland

Subud Britain
Southdown House
Golden Cross
Hailsham
E. Sussex BN27 4AH

Subud South Africa
P.O. Box 487
Melville 2109

Subud Canada
P.O. Box 92, Station H
Toronto
Ontario M4C 5H8

Subud U.S.A.
13701 Bel-Red Rd., Suite B
Bellevue, WA 98005

Subud Ireland
c/o Heaslip
Kilmoney
Carrigaline, Co. Cork

Contact addresses in other parts of the world are available from the International Subud Committee, which functions in a new country every four years or so. From January 1989 its address is:

International Subud Committee
Takatsu PO Box 40
Tawasaki-shi
Japan 213

Subud Publishers

Other books and publications about Subud are available from:

Subud Publications International Ltd. *(extensive list)*
Southdown House
Golden Cross, Hailsham
East Sussex BN27 4AH
England

Starlight Press *(two titles)*
GPO Box 2573
Sydney, NSW 2001
Australia

Undiscovered Worlds Press *(two titles)*
Suite 7, Box 17
1400 Shattock Avenue,
Berkeley, Ca. 94709
U.S.A.

Order Form

Dawn Chorus
419 N. Larchmont Blvd., Suite 22
Los Angeles, Ca. 90004

———————

Please send me _____ copy(ies) of *Revelation Subud*

I enclose ($8.95 per copy): $ _____

plus sales tax, 54¢ per copy: $ _____
            (Californians only)

plus shipping: $ _____
          $1.45 for first book & 60¢
          each addn'l book *(book rate)*

or $2.50 for first book & 50¢
          each addn'l book *(first class)* $ _____

                Total: $ _____

Please make check payabe to **Dawn Chorus**

Name _____

Address _____

_____

_____Zip _____

Phone _____